Romancing the Divine

Romancing the Divine

▲ ▲ ▲

The Art and Science of Falling in Love with God

Second Edition, 2017

Michael Henry Dunn

copyright 2018, all international rights reserved

ISBN: 1516861469
ISBN 13: 9781516861460

*Dedicated to my mother and father,
Kathryn Ann Dooley Dunn,
and Dr. Paul Joseph Dunn*

Table of Contents

Chapter 1	The Elusive Lover	1
Chapter 2	A Simple Practice of Love	3
Chapter 3	Birthday Dreams and Long Falls	5
Chapter 4	The Why of Love	8
Chapter 5	The Missionary New Age Church of Irish-Catholic Tribal Holistic Medicine	10
Chapter 6	The Love You Seek	13
Chapter 7	The Soul Mate Who Wasn't	17
Chapter 8	The Divine Mother	22
Chapter 9	The Dwarf's Door	25
Chapter 10	Overcoming the Enemies of Love	29
Chapter 11	Images of the Lover	36
Chapter 12	Choosing a Guide	40
Chapter 13	Psychic Sideshows	45
Chapter 14	Meditation-The Stillness of Love	49
Chapter 15	Meddling in the Occult	56
Chapter 16	Discipline	58
Chapter 17	The Pendant	62
Chapter 18	The Fire	65
Chapter 19	Escape from Monkey Island	68
Chapter 20	The Glittering Palace	78
Chapter 21	Marriage and Meditation	81
Chapter 22	The Lover's Presence	86
Chapter 23	The Lake Shrine	88
Chapter 24	Meditation and Money	93

Chapter 25	Years in the Monastery Kitchen	97
Chapter 26	The Lover to the Rescue	105
Chapter 27	The Restoration of Chivalry	116
Chapter 28	For Women: The Bride of God	122
Chapter 29	The Lover in Disguise	125
Chapter 30	Chanting and the Battle for Love	128
Chapter 31	Of Brother Bhaktananda's Bliss	136
Chapter 32	Saving the World	141
Chapter 33	Dark Night	146
Chapter 34	Back to Assisi…and On into Darkness	151
Chapter 35	The Lover in the World	156
Chapter 36	The Passing of Brother Turiyananda	160
Chapter 37	The Beloved and the Fear of Death	164
Chapter 38	The Reality of Bliss	169
	Appendix – Spiritual Resources	173

CHAPTER 1

▲▲▲

The Elusive Lover

My heart broke quite badly once, and I almost became a monk. I'd walked out on a treacherous limb for the wrong woman, and after it snapped cruelly, that mysterious longing emerged again, whispering of healing and hope. A family friend had a brother who was the abbot of a Trappist monastery in Iowa, and I almost surrendered my unfettered existence as a young actor for a life of silence, prayer, and hard work.

Almost.

But I wanted to believe that I could assuage that unignorable spiritual longing, and still love a woman. I wanted to believe that the thrills of the body and the joys of the heart could still leave room for the bliss of the soul. Though the lovely delusion of a soul mate had been shattered (for a time), the hope of union with the one I still hesitated to call "God" would not go away.

In later years, the once unthinkable names of "Goddess" and "Beloved" would fill my heart's prayers, but those days were a long way off.

An elderly nun laughed at me once, when I told her I couldn't make this hope for union with Source go away, and couldn't understand where it came from. But her laughter was light and sympathetic, and then she sighed, "Yes, there is no understanding it."

Now I am past the half-century mark, and I no longer try to understand or explain away this need to be in love with the Goddess who is God. Now She is as real to me as the desk at which I write. And though I would hover at the edge of monastic life for the better part of two decades, and though I would walk with saints and experience miracles, still I'm a man in the world, and I couldn't help loving Her in the human forms in which She came to me, in those two long marriages which I treasure and regret.

When these pages began to appear, a friend warned me that if words of divine love start to pour through you to share with others, you must look to be severely tested, and soon, on those themes of which you presume to speak. While the warning soon proved true, I didn't imagine that it would feel like a death, that I would experience cruelty, and also be called cruel, all in the name of loving Her in truth.

But at least I can now speak of the soul's dark night in something more than an academic sense. And at least now no one will mistake me for a saint. Or, if I become one through Her grace some day, I can serve as an encouragement to flawed and ardent lovers, an example for clucking tongues to say, "See! Even that fellow turned out well enough in the end!"

So I make no claim to a special grace or dispensation that qualifies me to share these stories. But neither am I an especially spectacular sinner. For reasons that remain mysterious to me, I have been blessed with a terrible thirst to know Her, and with years in the company of some few great souls who knew Her intimately. And I've been blessed (or cursed) with that storytelling compulsion of which Lincoln said, "I must tell these stories…or go mad."

CHAPTER 2

▲▲▲

A Simple Practice of Love

I HEARD A monk say once that he wanted to learn to listen well to others. His duties called for much counseling, and he found his attention wandering as hearts were poured out to him, found judgments creeping in as confessions were made to him. And so he came upon a simple practice which he shared with us. While looking into their eyes as they spoke, he mentally, silently, sincerely, and continuously affirmed the words, "I love you."

Silently. Sincerely. While listening.

And he found that everything changed. The beauty in their faces became clear to him, the air in the room subtly tingled with a higher vibration, their irritating quirks faded from his view (or became endearing foibles) and he could see a faint anxiety gradually vanish from their expressions - anxiety that had sprung from the half-conscious awareness that he hadn't really been listening to them. Now they felt heard, listened to, cared for. And the simple experience of talking with him suddenly had a healing dynamic of its own, unrelated to any counsel he offered or breakthroughs they achieved. All due to the silent power of those unspoken but deeply affirmed words.

I found it to be so as well. I began to experiment. At a restaurant, I turned to a middle-aged waitress, my eyes no doubt shining with the love I had been silently affirming to her, and she gave a visible start upon seeing the love in my eyes - not used to such expressions from her customers! And I found that my experience of that love was sincere - it was not a technique or a trick. By the sincere and deep affirmation of that phrase as I gazed at her, her inherent spiritual beauty became apparent to me, and my desire for her well-being became palpable to me - and so she saw it and felt it. And I ordered my food, and all was normal - but the encounter was uplifted, and joy had been generated.

"I love you…"

Man to woman, mother to child, friend to friend, they are the words we all long to hear. They express the reality we all long to experience. Why do we not think that God longs to hear them as well?

CHAPTER 3

▲ ▲ ▲

Birthday Dreams and Long Falls

MARK WELL ANY dreams you remember from the night before your birthday. The mind is aware of these cycles, and will sometimes send us messages that matter, harbingers of the year ahead, a blessing, or a warning.

Close to my fiftieth birthday, I dreamed I was flying. High in clouds and bathed in light, I sang as I flew and I was in bliss. I sang the "Ave Maria" of Bach and Gounod, and as I reached the climax of the song, as if the heat of my love had melted the wax that held my wings, I plummeted to earth in a dying fall.

I awoke from the dream at that moment and remembered two things: that at the moment I began my fall, I sang the Latin words *nunc et in hora mortis nostrae* ("now and at the hour of our death"). And that as I fell I saw in the sky enormous numerals - the number "52" carved in cloudy letters on the background of blue.

"Oh," I thought to myself, "so I will die at age fifty-two while singing the Ave Maria. That's not a bad way to go." But it gave me pause, as I was about to turn fifty, and was in no hurry to die.

I have not yet turned fifty-three as I write this, but I did die that year after all (in a way) and I was singing that prophesied phrase on the day itself. On my 52nd birthday I flew to Italy to sing the Ave Maria (and other devotional songs to the Divine Feminine) for a global gathering of monks and nuns from many faiths, in St. Francis' peaceful town of Assisi. And during that pilgrimage I decided to leave my marriage of many years, because the inner guidance was so clear. And I knew that I would deeply hurt a loved one, that few would understand my choice, that it would be seen in my community as a fall from grace, and that there were no guarantees of what awaited me after.

But the years of silent communion had made the Lover so real that I moved forward nevertheless, though I felt like Abraham leading his son Isaac to slaughter.

There is a wide green space in front of the massive basilica in Assisi where the bones of St. Francis are interred (in his last days, when this radically humble soul knew there was no preventing his disciples from erecting a massive church in his honor, he begged them at least to bury him among the criminals and the prostitutes – their once-dishonored graveyard at the far end of the town is now a place of pilgrimage).

Near the edge of the lawn in front of the cathedral there is a life-size statue of a knight on horseback. But it is not a triumphant image. The knight sits at a dejected angle, his whole attitude is one of brooding introspection, and even the horse seems dispirited, catching his rider's mood. A plaque set in the grass nearby tells the story. The young Francis (Francesco Bernadone was his name) dreamed of glory as a knight, and set out in costly gear to serve a local nobleman's war against neighboring Perugia. But two days out from Assisi, a crisis of the soul seized him, an angel appeared in a dream, and asked him, "why serve the servant, when you could serve the Master?" Caught up in the realization that his life's purpose lay in serving God, Francis implored in prayer, "what must I do?"

"Return to your city, and you will be shown what to do."

Romancing the Divine

St. Francis Basilica, Assisi, Italy

It was only on my last morning in Assisi, after a week of praying for guidance at his crypt at dawn every day, that I wandered over to the statue and read the story. Here (by all accounts) was one of history's greatest lovers – one who had, in truth, finally tasted the sweetness of the elusive Lover, if anyone had. I had come to his crypt hoping for some blaze of illumination that I could take home with me, some mystic message that would allow me to break a loved one's heart and somehow blame God. But there would be, after all, no fiery letters in the sky, and the decision would be mine, guided only by the ethereal touches of Her hand. And it came down to the simple message given to Francis. "Return to your city and you will be shown what to do."

I had a flight to catch in Rome that day, so that much was certain: I would be returning to Los Angeles, and somehow I would find a way to speak my truth. Through thirty years of seeking I had fallen in love with the Divine, and She had become real to me, but I would still have to stumble my way through karmic buzz saws the way we all do, hurting those I love the way we all do, knowing only that in the end we will all come home to Her.

CHAPTER 4

▲ ▲ ▲

The Why of Love

WHATEVER YOUR RELIGION, you are subject to the powerful pull of what Buddhists call The Ten Thousand Things – which is to say the World, the Flesh, the Devil, your laptop, your boss, your cell phone, your business, your lover, your friends, your spouse, your children, your regrets, your hopes, and your fears of dying unfulfilled. They vex you and they draw you, can still delight you, and they call to you night and day. And still you are reading this page – which may mean (we will suppose) you have always yearned for a higher love, most likely without knowing why.

I knew a monk who was once beset by such doubts. He lived in the daily presence of a saint now widely regarded as one of history's holiest men, but still his teacher was but a man, after all, and the monk had his doubts. He was a practical sort of fellow, had been a barber in Pittsburgh, and despite his growing bliss in meditation, at night he would toss and turn with doubts.

The Master spoke to him one day: "I see you spend your nights doubting." Startled (as he had spoken of it to no one), the monk replied, "Yes, sir – I can't seem to help it." "You should meditate more deeply," advised the guru. This went on for several weeks, with the Master accosting him now and again to say, "I see you still spend your nights doubting." "Yes, sir, it's true," he would say lamely.

One day the Master said, "I see you doubt still…THE DEVIL IS OUT OF YOU!!" The saint shouted this emphatically and the monk was quite startled. "That was very strange," he said to himself. "Why did he say that?"

Romancing the Divine

But he never doubted again. And in time he became...well, I will tell you more of him later.

You may not have an illumined teacher at hand to rewire the grooves of your brain's synapses with one power-charged affirmation, to help you overcome your need to know the "why" of love. But at least you can give yourself permission to love. And permission to give your desire for love the highest value – higher than any promise sung to you by the Ten Thousand Things.

CHAPTER 5

▲ ▲ ▲

The Missionary New Age Church of Irish-Catholic Tribal Holistic Medicine

I WILL NOT pretend to be more than I am: a flawed and irrepressible seeker. But neither will I pretend in false humility not to have been blessed with the company and guidance of great souls. Though I was born and raised a Catholic, and later accepted a great master of India as my guru, I only realized later in life that I had never really left the path into which I was born. It was a different kind of church, and not one easily labeled. It wore one kind of face in public (at Mass, and at St. Edmund's Grammar School), and a different one at home. If I had to label it now, I would call it The Missionary New Age Church of Irish-Catholic Tribal Holistic Medicine.

The tribal aspect were ten incessantly warring siblings, who yet regarded themselves as a race apart; the Catholic reality was standard catechism, sacraments, stern nuns, and devotion to sweet Mary; the Irish element was my mother's volcanic Celtic temper - daily eruptions that became a sort of semi-sacred family ritual; the New Age strain was my father's hatha yoga practice and my mother's insistence that we all be schooled in methods of clairvoyance (leading to my vain attempts to meet my brother Mark at midnight in the kitchen – but only in our astral bodies) – and the presence throughout our hulking Victorian twelve-bedroom home of books on yoga, reincarnation, and the work of Edgar Cayce; while the missionary holistic medical aspect was the passion of our parents' lives – a dedication to fulfilling their self-appointed role as the alternative healing court-of-last-resort for thousands of children with learning disabilities, brain injuries, and bio-chemical imbalances who would not otherwise have been helped - with a ready laboratory of their ten off-spring on whom to lovingly experiment.

The Dunn Family in the early 1970's (author at far right)

Now, rather than identifying with any church (though, in fact, I am a loyal member of a spiritual fellowship) I think of myself as just a lover who yearns to personally love (and be personally loved by) Divine Reality itself. But I was blessed with an environment which primed me to seek that love, schooled me in devotion to the Divine Feminine, taught me there were things in heaven and earth undreamed of by Sister Consolata Marie, and lifted me out of a parochial view of the destiny of souls.

But still as a young man I felt thwarted and unfulfilled, having learned enough to know that there had to be a method, had to be a teacher, but wary of the paths I had seen, the teachers I had read, and unwilling to surrender my questioning mind to the siren call of easy answers and the refuge of charismatic fundamentalism.

I had learned to demonstrate clairvoyant function (though I never did master the trick of meeting my little brother in the kitchen in our astral forms). I had dabbled in trance-channeling, had nearly been killed in a fire by a malevolent entity (more on that later), and had experienced fleeting and terrifying glimpses of past lives. My ego had been inflated and punctured three or four times, and I was working on the humility thing.

I had meandered through the bookstores and libraries of Chicago and New York, had read the Bhagavad Gita, and The Cloud of Unknowing, the work of Pierre Teilhard de Chardin, and the great mystical commentaries of Aldous Huxley, had developed a one-sided conversation with my Maker, and knew that to love as deeply as I yearned to love I needed a method, must somehow find the discipline to follow it, and would surely need a teacher to show me the way.

I dreamed one night of a Light at the head of the table at the Last Supper. I floated towards this beautiful light, arms outstretched in a transportment of yearning.

Let me go back a little. Before I met my Master, there was that matter of the broken heart, the treacherous limb, and the wrong woman.

CHAPTER 6

▲▲▲

The Love You Seek

It is the desire for union with irresistible beauty, the joy of silent companionship, the sublime assurance that you are loved beyond reason and without reason, the fore-knowledge of forgiveness for any and all trespass, a perfect trust in your lover's faith, a joy in each other's joy that thrills your soul, an ease of intimacy in all phases of life, a constant counselor, friend, and lover who never deserts you – even in death...

And yes, a Lover who may even one day make Herself known by touch, make Himself known by voice.

This is a love that all lovers seek, that all lovers yearn to offer, and that few of us ever experience. Being human, we cannot expect such love of those we love. We cannot promise to give such love to those we love.

But our hearts wouldn't yearn for it if it didn't exist. The Divine has planted the yearning in our souls, and the roots go to bedrock.

Only a little searching will reveal to you that there are those who have found the Lover. Only a little receptivity will draw to you the poems, the ecstatic writings, and (if your yearning is very strong) the living testimony of one who lives in the daily Reality of this love that seems so impossible.

And the true lovers of the Lover will warn you – this path is not easy. One lover I knew of said this upon finding the Lover:

Michael Henry Dunn

"The sublime splendor and joy of this discovery were so vast that...centuries, millenniums, countless eons of suffering were as nothing, as less than nothing, if by such means this bliss could be obtained."*

(Tara Mata, "Forerunner of the New Race", Self-Realization Fellowship, Los Angeles)

I believe you are closer to finding the Lover than millenniums! If you hadn't already endured countless eons of suffering, your desire for the Lover would not be awake, and you would not be reading this page.

However, the lovers of the Lover will also warn you of this: those who would walk this path will have enemies. That will need a chapter of its own...

For some, the very concept may offend: to be in love with God? To take the romanticism of love between man and woman, the draw of the sexes, the power of the erotic, and to apply this language, this imagery, this passion, to that God whom our Western heritage has for centuries seen only as the Father? To imagine a passionate lover's relationship, a direct, intimate, profoundly sweet and tender exchange, unmediated by any church or teacher or priest, that is yours and yours alone – to take your Lover's hand and hold it to your heart, to kiss the divine Hand in the night, and whisper as to your dearest love in the midst of your pain or your delight...some will say that this is sacrilege.

And if you are a man, to think of God as "Her" may even prompt you to hastily put this book down.

Or perhaps not. Perhaps the possibility that an intimate relationship to the Divine, direct and pure, is possible – perhaps this might lead you to linger here a little longer.

To those who may long for such intimacy, but feel qualms and a certain sheepishness, who yearn for and yet draw back from the sheer unabashed romanticism of it all, who may listen for the small still voice of intuition, and hear instead the small shrill voice of cynicism ...to those seekers, I would say this: look in the mirror.

Look into your own eyes and be present to the wonder of your soul looking back at you. Now close your eyes and imagine for a moment the face of your dearest friend, or of a great man or woman you love and admire, or the face of your child, or your lover, or the face of your beloved father or mother (if you were blessed to love them as I love mine), and imagine the most irresistibly gorgeous music washing over you as you gaze upon these beloved faces.

Then open your eyes and let yourself remember this: those loving and deeply loved faces, that soul-stirring beauty, all those images, music, and memories that move your heart most deeply: they all sprang into this world in the moment when a man and woman came together in love to create a new human being. In our human lives, there is nothing more sacred than that union.

To take that sacred moment, the experience of that love and to turn it toward God is the most natural motion the soul can conceive. For that union is but a paler reflection of the higher union of the soul with Spirit itself. And all one's life – whether we know it or not – is but the story of Spirit's loving pursuit of the soul, in the hope that someday we will turn and look back over our shoulder to behold the face of the One who has been yearning for our love.

It is my experience that if you follow the lover's path with heart, if you seek out the method of inner communion that works for you and the guide who is meant for you, if you do not let your flaws and stumbles deter you (even grave flaws, even disastrous stumbles), if you find that Image of the Divine that stirs your heart, if you whisper to that Lover ceaselessly and go within each day to commune with your Beloved in the silence, and carry that joy on into the battles of your day, then this sweetest of lovers will touch you, will guide you, will become unmistakably Real to you, will become Reality Itself to you.

Michael Henry Dunn

And all you need say to your inner cynic – and to those who might lightly mock the sight of this book in your hands – is this:

"I believe in Love....What do you believe in?"

CHAPTER 7

▲▲▲

The Soul Mate Who Wasn't

ONE OF THE blessings of growing up in The Missionary New Age Church of Irish-Catholic Tribal Holistic Medicine was the example of my parents' marriage. A word of inharmony between them was so rare as to constitute a historic event, a story to be retold with awe by us in later years ("Remember the time Dad told Mom she was acting like a child?"). Everything they did as parents had one thought – with two aspects: what is the best and most perfect thing we can do for our children? And how can our passionate missionary partnership incorporate this best and most perfect thing into our holistic pediatric practice?

In other words, they were soul mates on a mission.

As you may know, whatever model of marriage you grow up with will be the unseen screen on which you project your image of a future spouse.

The operative word here being "project."

In my early twenties I had returned to our home in Chicago after some rough years in New York City. I was already well and truly haunted by the desire for the Lover which prompted you to pick up this book. I had looked in vain for an example of anyone who had experienced this intimacy without embracing celibacy and seclusion. Being by nature a romantic, I was not the sort of person to whom celibacy was attractive, and the idea of romancing the Goddess Herself (had it occurred to me then) would likely have drawn a shudder of Catholic shame. Though I did not yet have an intimate concept of Source, I knew that my life would be empty without God, and feared that no woman would be happy with second place. The possibility of finding both seemed quite remote. I was not looking for, and did not really believe in, a soul mate.

In other words, I was obliviously waiting to be ambushed by the first plausible projection of the *anima* that came along.

A brief tale to make, I was drawn in to a love affair with a woman I met in artistic circles (let us call her Carrie). I had returned from something of an emotional wasteland in New York, and was starved for romance. We were working together on a creation of high-flown ideals, and so the promise of a mission hung in the air (it was only quasi-spiritual, but the verb here is "project," remember?). A sign of what was to come may have been given me by the fact that I disliked her on sight. Many an ill-fated affair has begun thus.

Suddenly, my genetic imprint and ancestral model kicked in, and all my passion for the Divine, for a life filled with beautiful purpose, was channeled towards, and projected onto the person of, this very human girl. I had fallen headlong into the lovely delusion of the soul mate.

The chemistry exploded into a blissful vision (not all of which I bothered to disclose to her): we would share a missionary passion for the theater; we would be artists, saints, and lovers; we would astonish the world even as we saved it, and we would make fabulous love until the end of time.

It ended badly.

More than badly, it ended excruciatingly. Upon the crash of it, I neither ate nor slept for several days. All the pain they sing about in the songs we love was suddenly real to me, and it was nothing to sing about. A clear choice lay before me. I knew that through sheer force of will I could overcome the obstacles in my path to win her back – at the cost of high damage to all involved. Or I could surrender the moment to the Divine, and rein in the rampant self-will that had exploded in my life.

Romancing the Divine

I cried very hard. I prayed very hard. I ate very little. I slept not at all.

In trying to explain away the ensuing miracle, I told myself it was the result of the fasting, or of the sleeplessness, of an overheated brain and an exhausted nervous system. But these moments of rationalization were fleeting, for the bliss was not to be trifled with, and swept away all petty defenses.

It happened like this: I remember standing in the window of my fourth-floor walk-up apartment on the North Side of Chicago, four days into the pain, facing west into the sunset, and making one more supreme effort of surrender to the unknown Lover of this misguided love that had wrecked my heart.

And suddenly all was well. All was very much more than well. Suddenly it didn't matter if Carrie came back to me, or if I ever found another. Joy flooded my heart without warning, a joy that was its own sweet reason for being. It filled my body from the heart outwards, and made breathing seem a frivolous distraction. I would have laughed aloud out of sheer amazement, but the bliss created its own intense silence and literally took my breath away.

This can't last, I told myself. But then bliss wiped out thought and my breath vanished again. This was the Lover, and She would not be denied. I walked out into the brisk winter air, and still it went on. For two full days this great joy would hover and then swoop down, dipping into my soul with great splashes of ecstasy.

Somehow I knew that life would go on, that the bliss would ebb from this height, and that I was not now a saint, nor even halfway recovered from a badly broken heart. I knew that I needed time to heal, and that I had much to learn.

But I had tasted the reality of the Love for which I had hungered.

I am not saying that your heart must be shattered for the Divine to break in – but it often seems to be so. Spirit is shy – or as my master put it, "God has an inferiority complex – He doesn't think much of Himself." He will wait until He is sure you really want Him in place of anything else, sure that you really are seeking His will for you, and not your own.

That will is not always easy to discern, and to seek it is not a matter of blind surrender, blind faith, and meek abnegation of the dynamic power of your mind and will to some unseen Dictator. The Lover gave you a mind with which to unravel Her maze, as well as a heart with which to love Her. And each lover's path to the Beloved is unlike any other, and I cannot say how yours will unfold. But the Lover will search out your heart to see if truly want Her love above any other.

Her love is perfect, you see, while ours, of course, is very much not so. And the Perfect Lover's one desire is for the beloved's joyful completion and happiness. If it is clear to the Lover that we believe there is greater joy to be found in the arms of another, She will turn aside and say, "I am joyful only in your own joy. I will wait."

I am not pretending I could easily manifest this degree of unconditional love today (if I should be blessed with a partner again in this life). I am only glad I haven't been given that excruciating test again – a test which She chose to send instead to one who loved me. But we are speaking of how She loves us, not of our imperfect attempts to love Her back.

Mind you, back in Chicago in my twenties, after the heartbreak and the bliss, I still wanted the girl. If Carrie had returned from Baja and left the other fellow, and asked me to give her again the mystical Irish ring she'd sent back, if she'd rekindled the dream, I would have fallen back at once into the exquisite pain of it all (and I very nearly did).

But my surrender had allowed some merciful grace to flow and I was spared from an immediate recurrence. And lest I paint too gallant a picture of myself for you, I will confess that after some months, after the bliss had indeed ebbed

Romancing the Divine

from its height, I sought out (as deeply wounded lovers often will) someone who would want me more than I wanted her, someone I knew would not leave me, so that I would not be hurt again at once. And so I unwittingly kindled another's hidden dream, and this new lover projected her yearnings onto me, as I had done onto Carrie – projected them onto one who could not fulfill them and who would before long break her heart, as mine had been broken.

I saw this clearly, and was haunted by the guilty certainty that I would hurt her. But more than this, I was haunted by the fleeting taste of blissful communion I had been given. And my new lover sensed that she had a Rival with whom she could not compete, while I secretly clung to my dashed hope that I might yet find both divine communion and human comfort.

But in that early haunted time, I was at last hungry enough, and desperate enough, and just purified enough, it would seem, to merit a dream of Light.

CHAPTER 8

▲ ▲ ▲

The Divine Mother

WE STAND IN such need of Her - the Compassionate, the Unconditionally Loving and Forgiving, the Intuitive, the Fertile, the Healing, the Nurturing — our world is withering for lack of these feminine qualities. And if these qualities do not speak to you of God then I recommend you, friend, to some other book! And if you would insist that Spirit wear only a masculine Face, a masculine Name, and come to us only as the Law-Giver, the Prime Mover, the Protector, the Creator, if you would restrict the nature of God to only these qualities, and regard Woman and Motherhood as secondary, earth-bound, and inferior — well, clearly, you are not likely to be reading this page!

You are with me this far, perhaps, because your intuition tells you that God's twin aspects of Feminine and Masculine, the Dance of Feeling and Reason, the intertwining of Nature and Spirit, the Divine Romance between the Soul and the Creator, answer a deeply felt need in your being.

If you are a woman, my task is easier — you need only look in the mirror to see Her. You need only cease for a moment to regard your body as merely a magnet for affection, and see it instead as our world's most perfect reflection of the abundance of nurturing Nature Herself. You need only cease to feel anxiety over enhancing the beauty of your eyes, and remember instead that men are really only drawn (if only we knew it) to the compassionate light of the Feminine that shines there. You need only cease to fear that your figure is not provocative, and remember instead that every man who is stirred by the sight of your sweet curves is only responding (unconsciously though it may be) to the memory Divine Mother planted in him of Her unforgettable beauty and perfect love - a memory echoed in this life by the dimly present recollection of the perfect contentment of the infant at the mother's breast. That driving and powerful memory is the secret behind evolution's procreative urge – the blind motive toward union that our animal natures have not yet matured enough to recognize as potentially the most angelic gift of our being.

That we men do not revere you as Her reflection is our tragedy.

And if you are a man, and this spiritually romantic yearning you feel is tethered to the demands of your reason, if your mind requires proof of the reality of God in the aspect of Divine Mother before you can reach out to Her as that Lover with Whom you are destined for union, then I would encourage you to become an empiricist of love, and to make the experiments of the heart that are offered in this book. If the promise of intimate communion with the Infinite is lure enough to earn your sincere effort, you shall have proof enough, if you persist.

Though my reason did demand (and find) a logical path towards the Goddess, I found finally that Her reality required no intellectual proof. The sun on my face became enough. The leap of my heart at the sight of an expanse of green meadow became enough. The way my cells felt gratitude for a drink of clear water became enough. The incomparable comfort of an embrace from the woman who gave birth to me became proof enough of the Mother from whom my mother came.

If seeing God as both Mother and Lover confuses you, then you may need to practice more reverence for the mother in the woman you love.

If you do so, you will find that every time Spirit tempts you with Her irresistibly seductive beauty, every time you feel Her caress in the breeze, or offer Her your heart in the silence of the night, you will find yourself falling in love with Her Divine Motherhood at the same moment that She comes to you in Spirit as the Divine Lover.

And if She has also come to you in mortal form as the woman you love, then you are doubly blessed.

And if you are a woman who is drawn to women, or a man who is drawn to men, in a way your path may be easier, for the blending of Masculine and Feminine between you and your mortal lover may offer you (more so, perhaps, than for opposite-gender lovers) a greater chance to see each other first as souls, and only secondarily as identified with these bodies we inhabit. And the Divine may then come to you in vision (perhaps) in whatever form your heart holds dear.

CHAPTER 9

The Dwarf's Door

It was in that same fourth floor walk-up on Chicago's North Side that the dream came. It was perhaps a year later. The bliss had long faded and my heart was well toward healing, but the memory of it haunted me. I was busy but not happy. I had been shown that the Love I sought was real, but I had no path back to it — and four days of sleepless heartbroken fasting was not a formula I cared to repeat.

You may have had dreams in which there is no preamble and no back story - just an image, indelible and steeped in deep emotion, that brings you awake in the night. That is how this was for me: I dreamed my way into an iconic painting. I became a figure at the table in Dali's "Last Supper," and at the head of the table shone a Light, bright, gentle, and so full of Love that my body lost its density on the instant, and rose in the air to accompany my heart in its flight Home.

I don't have such dreams often. At that time, I had never had such a dream.

It might have been the next day, or the day after. Wanting to visit my parents, I drove out to the old hulking tribal manse (still well-stocked with a few of the notoriously slow-to-mature Irish-American siblings - Irish Catholics tell the following joke, but do not allow others to tell it: how do we know Jesus was Irish? Simple: at age thirty-three, He had no job, He lived at home…and His mother thought He was Jesus Christ).

There was nothing profound on my mind, and I sat down in the kitchen to fix myself a snack.

Michael Henry Dunn

I have always been an obsessive reader. My mother taught me to read at a very young age, and time spent eating alone without something to read has always seemed to me time wasted. So there I sat, my sandwich hot and ready to eat, my many siblings not in evidence, and I looked around the kitchen for something to read, something to feed mind as well as body.

There was a bookshelf above the radiator – old copies of *National Geographic* and some other magazines. No, I thought, not that. I walked into the breakfast room – four full shelves of books: *Prevention* magazine – lots of those – books on how not to get cancer, old *Readers Digests,* a miscellany of *World Books' Book of the Year.* No, I thought, I need something better tonight. On to the former playroom we now called The Office – many books there. I plowed quickly through them all. "No, not that. This one won't do. Not that. Something better. No, not that."

I had become obsessed and my sandwich was now quite cold.

It was a large house, and had always had many books in its many rooms. When there are ten children who have each been given their own bedroom so that they might grow up to become truly cantankerous, self-engrossed, and eccentric members of The Missionary New Age Church of Irish-Catholic Tribal Holistic Medicine, over a quarter century or so such a home will accumulate a goodly and eclectic store of books.

The Dunn Family home at 333 N. Euclid in Oak Park, Illinois

Romancing the Divine

Down to the basement – three bedrooms. Books musty and mildewed, of dubious provenance. Nothing there. Back up to the second floor, five bedrooms there, all with bookshelves – surely in the Study (the bedroom of my teenage years) there would be something. *Gibbon's Decline and Fall of the Roman Empire?* No, it's just a sandwich, not a three-day banquet.

By the time I impulsively ran up the stairs to the five bedrooms on the third floor, I should have realized something strange was going on. Yes, I love to read and all that, but I'm usually fine with yesterday's paper, or even a book I've read a dozen times, just to content my eyes with passing over the written word.

I may have sprinted up the stairs with the intuition that there was one room on the third floor that was sure to hold some one book that might meet my strangely high standards this particular night - my oldest brother's room. It had briefly been mine one summer, and his closets were crammed with books. Chris majored in history, had an interest in politics, and worshipped Churchill. That would be my salvation.

But no. Churchill was there, but he would not do. Many dozens of titles were quickly glanced through, and all discarded. I was now on my knees in front of his closet, worn out with my weird search, surrounded by a pile of apparently unworthy books.

The Lover will occasionally require some eccentric behavior of you. Not always, but sometimes.

And then my eye fell on what we called The Dwarf's Door. In the far corner of the room, it was perfectly proportioned to be the stately entrance to a manor, but it was only two feet tall, and led to a closet that might have held a wardrobe for a hobbit, but could accommodate only a few dozen human-sized books. I crawled over, opened the door (as a child I'd always done so in terror of dwarves), and went through my last due diligence in this fevered search.

Michael Henry Dunn

I discarded them all. Save one.

The last book, on the last shelf. A very slim volume, no more than five inches high, with its title facing away. I had to pry it out of its hiding place and turn it round to see what it was.

Now, I promised you that I am not here as a proselytizer for any one teacher or path. Yes, I've brought you a long way up to this third floor bedroom, and built up a lovely suspense as to what marvelous book could have been the sequel to so powerful a dream (don't worry, you'll find it in the list of Lover's Resources at the back of this book).

But, you see, if I tell you now what book it was, this little story I've told you will become all about that book and its author, who became my incomparable guru. But what I really want to share with you is that there may be one path, and someday, perhaps, one special teacher, one lovingly chosen route that the Lover has mapped out for you in your journey home, and no other will do. And it may not be the one that waited for me behind the Dwarf's Door. But it is surely waiting for you somewhere. You just have to be willing to discard all the others, and follow that one alone.

CHAPTER 10

——————— ▲▲▲ ———————

Overcoming the Enemies of Love

THIS IS A book of Romance, a book of sweet seductions, a book of loving arts, and divinely provocative images. But I cannot in conscience invite you into it without sharing an unblinking look at the opponents of Love, or we will come to grief.

I know a funny monk. The Reverend Mother of the order won't let him give sermons, because everyone in the temple would just laugh all through the service, and no one would meditate (he was an actor before entering the monastery, and entertaining is in his blood, so he must not be blamed). And this monk who is so funny will often say a serious thing to you with a jolly face, trying to lift your spirits:

"Just remember — you're swimming upstream!"

He says this, and then he laughs merrily, as if he's explained it all for you.

As he has in fact. For when you seek this love we've spoken of, this love you can't seem to live without, then you have dived into a vast river, and have turned upstream, determined to swim against the accumulated tributaries of the River of Life itself. Very nearly all of humanity swims the other way, drifting in the deep swift current, content to live and die in the spell of the Ten Thousand Things. All the world is a torrent heading away from Source, out into infinite manifestation, Spirit playfully tying itself to identification with Form. That the hidden goal of the vast game is to reach the moment you have reached (that moment when Love asserts Her primacy and begins to draw you back) - this is a secret that few know and fewer still want to hear. The derision of those adrift in the current is only one of the obstacles in your path.

For you have awakened from the spell, and have turned back to seek the Source of the river. You are brave to do this. Here are some of the opponents you will confront:

To Be Worthy of Love

> *"I think it is appropriate to tell you how I perceive myself before God, whom I behold as my King. I consider myself as the most wretched of men. I am full of faults, flaws, and weaknesses, and have committed all sorts of crimes against my King. In deep regret I confess all my wickedness to Him. I ask His forgiveness. I abandon myself in His hands that He may do what He pleases with me."*
>
> - Brother Lawrence, "The Practice of the Presence of God"

In this supposedly new age in which we dwell, unblinking introspection has a bad name. Consciousness of guilt and shame are to be shunned as psychological perils. And it is true – they are obstacles to love. Yet we see in the words above that one of the Divine's simplest-hearted and most blissful lovers, an obscure monastery kitchen-worker in 17th century Paris, was acutely conscious of his failings, and daily surrendered them to his Beloved.

That was his secret. He saw himself as he was, and gave himself to God in simple love.

And the daily miracle of his joy sprang from the astounding fact that the Lover received and rewarded him with intimacies of indescribable sweetness:

Romancing the Divine

My King is full of mercy and goodness. Far from chastising me, He embraces me with love. He makes me eat at His table. He serves me with His own hands and gives me the key to His treasures. He converses and delights Himself with me incessantly, in a thousand and a thousand ways. And He treats me in all respects as His favorite. In this way I consider myself continually in His holy presence.

My most usual method is this simple attention, an affectionate regard for God to whom I find myself often attached with greater sweetness and delight than that of an infant at the mother's breast...I would call this state the bosom of God for the inexpressible sweetness which I taste and experience there. If, at any time, my thoughts wander from this state from necessity or infirmity, I am presently recalled by inward emotions so charming and delicious that I cannot find words to describe them.

We need not be perfect to begin to practice love. We need not be perfect to deserve a perfect love. The Lover has created a world in which the consequences of our errors will chase us into Her arms, where even the most wretched of us will someday we embraced as the favorite child of Her heart. It is such a mystery! The Lover has flung the World into being with the joyful shout of the Primal Explosion, and trapped us in the ever-expanding echoes of that shout... and yet there is always the secret whisper of Love calling us home.

Waywardness

To be sure, there are laws to the Lover's world. Though the mystic's grand romantic passion can be found as a common aspect of all the great religious paths, so too we will find in every one of them the guidelines, the moral foundations, the commandments, the *namas* and *niyamas*, the do's and don'ts that are meant to safeguard the soul. If these are flouted, with no effort made at self-correction, we will find our path to the Lover blocked at every turn by the chaos we create in our lives.

I knew a young man who was entranced by the promise of bliss, of higher states of consciousness, of yogic powers. He threw himself with enthusiasm into the practice of meditation. After some progress, he found himself frustrated and distracted. It was his good fortune to have as his counseling monk our doubting friend, the former barber from Pittsburgh, who now lived a life of quiet bliss and service. It came to light that the young man was carrying on multiple affairs with various women. The monk advised him that this was the source of his difficulty, and that he must change his ways if he wished to progress in meditation.

"But, Brother!" the young man protested. "I want to be a yogi – not a saint!"

The monk smiled. "Good luck!" he said.

The Lover's laws are simple after all. We all know them. They all spring from the golden guideline: treat others as you would be treated.

We need not be perfect – but the intimacy of this Love will remain elusive if we are not making every effort to bring our lives into alignment with truth.

And if our efforts are in vain? If, despite our longing for the Divine, we are mired in self-destructive habits over which we seem powerless?

Take some comfort here: if you are subject to addiction in some form, you are in good company, for many great lovers of Spirit found the Lover through the struggle to escape from this most formidable enemy of love.

Addiction

My guru was building a new temple in Los Angeles in the 1940s. He had a disciple who was a skilled carpenter, and the carpenter loved the Master very much. But the carpenter could not stop drinking. He was deeply ashamed of this, but his love overcame his shame. Drawn by his devotion, he came to the building site one day to help the Master – even though he was quite drunk…and soon he broke down weeping at his weakness.

But the Master consoled him. "Don't try to be perfect first. Just keep meditating. Practice the meditation I have taught you, even if you have your beads in one hand and your bottle in the other. If you never give up, then one day your joy in God will overcome your bad habit, and you will be free."

And so he did. And so he was.

Is it so simple? Yes, it is.

And if you do not have an illumined teacher nearby, then Spirit may come to you in the form of a sober friend guiding you to support and recovery. Or as a loved one who intervenes. Or in the meetings where those of all faiths or none seek help from a Higher Power.

Those who seek this love we speak of often become trapped by addiction, because we are seeking something transcendent, some substitute for the Lover, some heightening that provides escape from the source of pain. Whatever form it may have taken, that pain is, in its origin, rooted in the agony of separation from our source.

So whether you have sought release in alcohol, or drugs, or sex, or destructive relationships, and regardless of whether you are still consumed by shame and seemingly caught forever in the grip, do not ever believe that you are unworthy of the Lover.

It is simply a matter of believing that you are loved - and never giving up.

Michael Henry Dunn

Distractions

Because you have chosen to swim upstream in search of Love, the world by its very nature will conspire against you. There is a science to Love as well as an art, and the Lover hovers over your practice of this science, waiting eagerly for the moment when your heart is clear and still and prepared for communion. But how can you prepare your heart for stillness, clarity, and the presence of the Lover in this world of chaos, distractions, duties, debts, family love and family labors, and the seemingly inescapable torrent of information and messages that technology has unleashed upon us?

This is not a world in which the art or the science of Love is easily practiced.

That is why in all times and places men and women have sought solitude and celibacy, simplicity and silence in spiritual communities where the search for the Divine may proceed undistracted.

But this is not a book for the celibate and the secluded. This is a book for those of us who have chosen to be in the world – and are yet longing for the intimate presence of Spirit - for those of us with family duties, and for those of us seeking human love as well as divine.

I can offer you no simple formula that will assure you of balance amid chaos. The multiplying complexities of our age are an insidious antagonist of this path. We are urged to seek simplicity in our lives – and this will help. Reduce our needs and wants – this too can bring serenity.

But I do not know of your challenges, burdens, griefs, and dangers, and words about the wisdom of simplicity may seem a pitiless jest when life presses hard upon you.

So I will only tell you what I know for certain: take the Lover's hand. Even if you don't yet believe it can be so, reach out in simplicity and ask for help. Whether in a garden or on the street, as you walk your ways make the silent

Romancing the Divine

gesture. Open your hand and place it in the hand of your Beloved who walks beside you. Make a habit of this. And you will find in time that amidst the chaos and stress there is a palpable Presence to comfort you, to guide you.

It may not come easily or soon, but if you persist, and if you call in simplicity from your heart, your Lover will respond – in a way you cannot deny, in a way that fills you with secret joy. What way the Lover will choose is for you to discover. Each romance with this Lover is unlike all others, and I will not presume to tell you how yours will unfold.

You must not give up - you are setting out to charm the Power that moves the galaxies! And as your faith in Love's response grows strong, all the weapons of the enemies of Love will prove weak in the presence of the One who holds your hand.

CHAPTER 11

▲ ▲ ▲

Images of the Lover

I PROMISED YOU a book of "sweet seductions" and one of the sweetest is the preparation of a trysting place to which you invite your Beloved.

You may live in a mansion or a flat, a bungalow or a barracks or a prison cell, but the creation of a private and sacred space for divine communion is essential. If you are not able to devote a whole room for this purpose, then find a corner and screen it off from view. Approach it as you would the preparation of a boudoir for your wedding night: this must be a place of inviting beauty and peace.

Let it be clean, with fresh air from a window if you can, and create a comfortable resting place – a chair or cushion – and cover it with a clean blanket of wool that runs under your feet, and above that a cloth of silk. Let it face east, if possible. There is a science to this love and facing east is part of it. Experimenters in consciousness have found over the centuries that silk and wool shield the devotee from powerful earth currents that pull the consciousness downward, and that facing east aligns you with the magnetism of the planet in a spiritually beneficial way. Believe this or not, as you like. You may find it to be true.

Images of the Beloved

Choose for your altar some image, or several, that particularly appeal to your heart. If you are drawn to Christ, find that image of Him that most touches you, and place it so that you and the Son of Man are gazing into each other's eyes.

If you are of India, focusing your love upon an adorable image of God may be easy for you – if also bewildering! – for your tradition has such an infinite variety of God's aspects from which to choose.

If you spring from Judaic or Islamic traditions and the use of a human image as a focal point for adoration is foreign to you, then find a way to beautify your altar, whether with fresh flowers or a decorative pattern, in a way that lifts your spirits and draws you to the spot.

Or if, like many in our age, you were not brought up in one strong tradition or church, you may wish to blend traditions, to have Christ and Krishna side by side, or the Virgin Mary twinned with Goddess Lakshmi, or a beloved photograph of a revered spiritual teacher.

Spirit Transcending Form

A gathering was held at the *ashram* of Paramahansa Yogananda, the great illumined Master of India. In keeping with the tradition of the Swami Order, the Master wore his lustrous black hair long, and it framed the angelic tenderness of his features in a way that heightened his innate beauty and made it seem almost feminine, while the power and nobility of his brow spoke of masculine strength. Across from him at the table that evening sat a young girl five years of age. Fascinated by this mysterious being, the child blithely interrupted the Master's conversation with a disciple to innocently enquire, "Are you a man or a woman?"

Michael Henry Dunn

Paramahansa Yogananda

"Neither!" replied the Master, and resumed his talk.

So Spirit might answer if we sought to limit Spirit's qualities to our mortal human roles.

Talk with Me

The Divine, as with any lover, craves your attention, feels joy when you gaze on him, yearns for time with you alone, and delights to hear you speak his Name. And Spirit's yearning for us, the Divine desire for our love, his great hope for our bliss, are (the great lovers tell us) of an intensity we can scarcely conceive.

When we first begin our tentative steps toward this love, when we first nurture the hope that this sacred intimacy might actually exist, we may feel drawn almost against our will, impelled by a longing we do not understand. It may feel as if we have awakened from a coma to find our memory gone, opening

Romancing the Divine

our eyes again to gaze with bewilderment into the eyes of a lover who knows us to our depths, who has been every day at our side, but whom we cannot remember. All that remains to us is the intuition, the soul-memory that we were loved once with a love so deep our very cells have retained the imprint. And somehow we must begin again, to revive and restore, to recall the sweet familiarity we once enjoyed with this stranger who is gazing on us with a look of such powerful love.

That is what your altar is for.

But the quietness of your altar is only a prelude to the quietness of your soul – that inner place of stillness where your romance with God may begin.

CHAPTER 12

▲▲▲

Choosing a Guide

THEY SAY THERE are no accidents. But then they also say that you must forge your own destiny. They say that when the pupil is ready, the teacher will appear. But then they also say that you must wisely discriminate true paths from false, and choose a teacher based on reason and intuition. They say that we choose our parents before we are born. But then they also say that at the moment of conception there is a flash in the ether, and many souls rush in that instant toward that newly fertilized human embryo, intent on securing this chance for rebirth.

And lovers in love cannot help but believe that destiny brought them together. But is it possible that the weight of your karma comes to the balance of a hair, and that you and your destined beloved might miss each other — take the wrong bus that day, miss the traffic light, skip what would have been the unforgettable dance, and lose what could have been a lifetime of love? Is the same true of the destined path and the chosen teacher that await those who would fall in love with God? Or do chance and free will take a hand?

Einstein feared to believe that "God plays dice with the Universe." I think She does, and that nevertheless Her children's bliss is assured, once we turn firmly towards Her.

So you might say the game is fixed but we have free choice, which we then use to forget that the game is fixed in our favor.

The Reverend Mother of a certain monastic order — the same order that schooled my sainted friend from Pittsburgh (his name was Brother

Bhaktananda) – counseled a troubled young monk one day. The Reverend Mother, Sri Daya Mata, was a direct disciple of that same great Master (the renowned Paramahansa Yogananda) who banished Brother Bhaktananda's doubts, and was herself a wonderfully holy person.

The young monk was very discouraged. For all his struggles he seemed to make no progress in meditation, he had vexing difficulties with his work in the monastery, and did not feel the bliss of Spirit as his daily companion. He did not doubt the reality of Divine Love – he simply felt that he was unworthy of it, and so he confessed, "Ma, I just don't think I'm going to make it."

She laughed out loud, heartily and long. When she got the better of her mirth, she told him, "My dear boy, you have no choice in the matter! Your guru is too great! You are going to be dragged kicking and screaming into heaven!"

So it might be said of all of us. Once we turn firmly toward the Beloved, once we recognize our need for a guide on the path, once we determine that we will never give up, the way home will not be long, and She will guide us to that place or that teacher destined for us.

Sanctity and Sainthood

Hale, holy, healthy, whole, holiday – they all spring from the same linguistic root. Holiness is nothing more than the most intense form of health possible to us: a complete integration of the soul with its blissful Source, the achievement in a given human being of the loving purpose for which the world was created.

Recognizing a saint, however, is not always easy. There were those in daily contact with Jesus Christ who failed to recognize His divinity.

And there will always be those who achieve a reputation for sanctity that exceeds their actual possession of it. The ochre robe of the East does not confer deep spiritual realization anymore than the clerical collar of the West.

Christ said: "By their fruits shall you know them."

Does the spiritual guide live the principles he teaches? Does he uphold and observe the universal precepts of morality that are the foundation of the Lover's path? Is he or she an example in their being and daily demeanor of the love, joy, and humility that you wish to experience? Do you intuitively sense when in their presence that they are sincere in what they teach?

And what of those others who follow a given teacher? Do they show reverence for her? Are there at least a few who are themselves joyful and holy?

This is not a choice anyone else can make for you, or an awareness that anyone else can create for you. Remember, it is the Lover you are seeking. Any teacher is merely a guide to Spirit, not a substitute for Spirit. And you may have many teachers, but there is only one Lover.

Prophets and Pretenders

Beware of the sensational, the seemingly supernatural, and the charismatic. Too often they offer a brief dazzlement, and seek to cement your attachment to themselves, rather than to guide you in humility towards your own intimate and direct communion with God. If you are impressed by one who can materialize flowers out of thin air, I would suggest your time might be better spent in seeking a florist!

Your religion does not matter if you are seeking the Lover. The great saints of all religions who experienced the bliss of the Divine Romance are testimony enough.

You need not believe that there are those rare souls who achieve complete Identity with Spirit. You need not believe that such a great lover can be a channel for Divine Love itself. You need not lessen your devotion to

Romancing the Divine

Christ (if He is your path) to hear that other great souls became Sons of God, Daughters of God.

But if it is your blessing to encounter such a one, you may look for these signs to recognize them: perfect humility, perfect purity, perfect bliss.

If they are truly humble with the humility of Spirit, they will point you only toward Spirit, never toward themselves.

If they are pure with the purity of Spirit, their lives will be an unstained example of spiritual living.

And rarest of all, if they are one with Spirit, they will manifest perfect bliss. This is not subjective! This love is a science. This bliss can be proven, tested, made known. For in the heights of divine union, breath ceases, heartbeat ceases, and the unwinking gaze is fixed on the eternal home of the Spiritual Eye, as the soul experiences Oneness with the omnipresent Cosmic Consciousness of God.

And being One with the omniscient, omnipresent, and eternal Lover, the love of such a one for you as a disciple will not be limited by time or space. As Christ came centuries after His earthly life to guide St. Francis (and as He still comes to those who love Him), so such a one can come to you.

For myself, I know this to be so, because my one saving grace is that I don't give up, and while I am far from the heights reached by my holy friends, I can tell you from my heart that it is so. You may discover the truth of it for yourself if you will.

You need not believe this. If it troubles you, let it go. The Lover will still find a way to draw you close. You may just have made His work a little harder, and it may take a little longer.

Well, to be honest, quite a lot longer. But the fix is in, remember? Your part is simply never to give up until you are in His arms.

CHAPTER 13

▲▲▲

Psychic Sideshows

THE RETROSPECTIVE VIEW of a spiritual quest (once you've gotten past the really awful stuff) assumes a sort of golden inevitability. The extended periods of agonized confusion, the disastrous detours, the profound doubts, the times of outright despair all seem to take on an aura of destiny, resolving into a pleasing picture of a divinely ordained march towards peace and bliss - when viewed with the reflective backward glance of one's middle years.

So it seems to me now, at any rate. It's all very well for me to rhapsodize for you now about divine intimacy, but what about the years spent caught in the fruitless fascinations of psychic phenomena? It is inspiring to read of many years of disciplined meditation, but what about the seven years of struggle before I even started? The sober and serene environment of the monastery seems like a beckoning haven in which to escape the addictive modern society, but will stories of encounters with saints be of any help to you at all if I gloss over my own frailties?

We are all a bit weary, I suspect, of well-meant books that offer the shorter route to enlightenment, the quicker path to bliss or wealth or love. The truth is that the path to the Lover is for most of us a long one. It's a long corridor with a sure Light at the end....and many tempting doors and seductive side paths that beckon as you go.

I'm not speaking to you from inside the Light. (Later on, I will happily direct you to those who can). But I've slipped or staggered past many of the tangent paths, and though I've peered curiously into an open side door or two,

I dare to believe that She's reeling me in steady and sure at this point. The immediate witness I can offer is that the Lover walks with you, and will hold your hand even from the early steps. This is not, in my experience, merely a lovely sentimental image. I speak of a physically tangible, undeniable sensation and presence that I long ago stopped trying to deny. The reality of that comforting intimate Presence is astonishing and heartbreaking, and when you feel those unexpected spontaneous touches of love and compassion, you may weep.

But we were speaking of the side paths, the temptations. No less a saint than the ecstatic Teresa of Avila wrote of how, in her early years of prayer, she would descend from hours of cloistered communion, from blissful intimacy with the Majesty of Heaven, and fritter away hours in idleness and trivialities in the convent parlor (in those days in sixteenth century Spain, convents were used by aristocratic families as temporary holding houses for unmarried daughters, who would be courted by potential husbands in the convent itself). And there, the woman who had minutes before been in the "Presence of His Majesty," would feel the bliss ebb away in the shallows of gossip.

But neither did she allow herself to become mired in guilt and self-recriminations. "To wish to act like angels while we are still in this world is nothing but folly," she told her nuns.

St. Teresa would finally find her own reputation for sanctity a burden, and implored God to prevent her frequent experiences of levitation in prayer, which were so distracting to others, and which brought her before the Inquisition as a suspected witch. But when her heart became suffused with the ecstatic love of God and raised to celestial bliss, her body would inevitably follow.

The Psychic Sideshows

Authentic spirituality and the company of the Lover have almost nothing to do with psychic phenomena, but the two are easily confused in the popular mind. In the beginning of my search the exotic novelty (to my young Catholic eyes) of reincarnation, past-life memories, ESP, the prophecies of Edgar Cayce, the titillations of Ouija boards, séances, and the trance-channeled voluble pseudo-sageliness of discarnate entities featured in the "Seth Speaks" books – all these beckoned as I attempted to shake off the shackles of catechism, and free my soul for love.

In our house, the Pope was revered, Sunday Mass was mandatory (though nearly always embarrassing, as the ten Dunn children would stagger in late and unignorable to the crowded church), the sacraments of the Church were duly administered, and we would gather in my parents' bedroom for evening prayers and blessings. So to the outside world, we appeared conventional Catholics.

But inside the red brick walls of 333 N. Euclid, apostasy was brewing. My respectable pediatrician father began to practice Hatha Yoga and grew a trim beard. A book by an Indian saint appeared on my parents' bathroom shelf featuring a face of transcendent bliss – a book that would one day change my life, but which, strangely (ravenous reader of mystical material though I was), I never opened as a boy. A bestseller by a Tibetan lama utterly fascinated me with tales of tortuous spiritual trials, the surgical opening of the all-seeing Third Eye, and secret underground lakes beneath vast Himalayan monasteries.

(Well, the author claimed to be the soul of a Tibetan lama, explaining that while he was, to outward appearance, a middle-aged Englishman, this was because his Tibetan body had gotten thoroughly beaten up, and he had to jump into a mature English body in mid-stream to save time. Please remember that I was only twelve years old – and for all I can attest, perhaps his story was true).

By the time the 1970's rolled in, it was only natural that my parents should decide to enroll us all in an intensive Mind Control course, where we were schooled in ESP, self-anesthesia, remote psychic diagnosis and healing of others' ailments, access to inner counselors, and methods of altering one's own brain-wave frequency. It was refreshingly practical (how to wake oneself up on time without a clock, how to dull pain from an injury until you could get to a doctor, how to make two hours sleep feel like eight, how to "program" your mind to achieve your goals), and for a teenage boy, it was a certified initiation into the essential New Age axiom that all was indeed possible if one simply focused on "creating one's own Reality."

But one question lingered for me. Our instructor told us that if we "programmed" intensely for the achievement of a goal, while performing practical actions to facilitate its realization, and if at length it finally refused to manifest, that the founder of the course had realized this meant your chosen goal "was not in accord with the Cosmic Plan."

Would it not make more sense, I thought, if one focused from the start on getting into alignment with this mysterious "Cosmic Plan," instead of engaging in an endless hit-or-miss pursuit of possibly fruitless goals?

St. Teresa would have called it opening one's soul to the will of God:

"All that the beginner in prayer has to do — and you must not forget this, for it is very important — is to labor and be resolute and prepare himself with all possible diligence to bring his will into conformity with the will of God."

But I was not a sixteenth-century Spanish nun, but a teenage boy in suburban Chicago. And while an altruistic idealism was the constant theme of my home life, a passionate quest for what Aldous Huxley called "the unitive love-knowledge of the Divine Ground of All Being" was not a dinner table topic. I had not yet merited a monastic environment. And it was the 70's, and I was an aspiring actor fascinated with past lives and Tibetan yogis and prophecies of coming apocalypse.

CHAPTER 14

▲▲▲

Meditation-The Stillness of Love

THE INTIMATE CONVERSATION you will have with the Divine can take place anytime and anywhere, for this Love is not limited by time and space. She is as close as you allow Her to be. And though it will be in times of quiet solitude, in places still and full of beauty, that you may experience your deepest communion, the miracle of this Lover is that She will often surprise you with a loving touch amid the din of crowds, when you are with those who know Her not at all, engaged, it may be, in activities mundane and tiresome, or even when you are succumbing to habits that draw you away from Her.

But before that can happen, it is my experience that you must convince Her first that you truly long to be Hers alone. You must whisper your love to Her with deep sincerity, when your mind and body are still, your attention focused on Spirit alone. The bond you will create together must begin in silence, and in deep prayer, and in that quiet that comes only with meditation.

Meditation

The word is now used for a dizzying variety of methods, from a hundred different paths, and is used to sanctify or elevate practices far afield from communion with Spirit, and may seem almost meaningless to the beginner on the Lover's path.

I will use the word simply to describe an ancient science of love. Meditation is that special form of concentration in which we turn our ardently focused mind and heart upon God alone.

Michael Henry Dunn

Other paths will use the word differently. Those drawn to Zen will find that meditation is centered on growing awareness of Non-Duality. Various yoga practitioners will use the word narrowly to describe certain breathing techniques, or *pranayama* exercises. I use the word as Paramahansa Yogananda used it, to describe the path of scientific yet divine Romance of which he was a supreme Master.

I promised I would share with you only what I know first hand, and I will not pretend to be a master of this science (thought I have practiced it for many years). And some of what I know I will choose not to share, for your path may prove different from mine, and I promised to honor Her secrets, and She may choose to reveal ways to you that are hidden from me, and may come to you through some other channel, chosen for you alone.

But this much you may already know: it is a science of breath, of awareness, a means of stilling both body and mind, calming the unquiet thoughts, so that you may begin to sever your identity with your body, and know yourself as the soul.

All your troubles and all the inner longing that impelled you to seek the Beloved in the first place, spring from your delusion that you *are* your body, and are due to the iron lock of ego on the cage where your soul is imprisoned. In the stillness of meditation, as the breath and heartbeat grow quiet, and as the thoughts are stilled, you begin to know your true nature as peace, as joy, as love, and in the highest states as the ever-new bliss of union with your Beloved.

For that is God's hidden nature as well. Behind enchanting gifts to you of beauty in this world, behind disguises as your loving friends, seen in adored reflections in the holy places where His children worship Him, God is, in essence, Being itself, Awareness itself, Bliss itself, Love itself.

And so are you.

Romancing the Divine

First Steps on the Inner Path

A quiet and unobtrusive monk, Brother Bhaktananda became an incarnation of Bliss, a humble minister whose spiritual greatness was known only to a few. He was an old man when I first met him, an outwardly unimpressive fellow, but he was one with the Beloved and the Presence shone through his eyes. His days of doubt were long gone, and the state of bliss in which he moved was so intense that you could actually feel the scorching field of joy around him - so much so that if he quietly sat down behind you, you knew without looking that it could only be him.

And if you would require miracles of one called a saint, he manifested those too — but you usually had to look carefully to detect his humble hand in the matter. Water into wine, no — a quietly miraculous pitcher of carrot juice was enough for Brother, from which he would unobtrusively pour some twenty glasses from a container sufficient to hold only six.

Healings, yes, those too — from a distance, and only in such a way so that the healing would be seen to come (as it truly did) from the hand of his Beloved.

One of his great challenges was to continually find ways to hide the intensity of his bliss, and to prevent any ostentatious manifestations of it, though it seems he could sometimes forget that others did not live in the same expanded cosmos in which he walked. Once he sat down behind me and a friend in the social hall as a rehearsal was in progress. My friend saw him, and turned, saying, "Oh, Brother, I'm sorry, am I blocking your view?"

"No, that's all right," he said simply. "I can see right through you."

When curious newcomers would gather on Thursday night after devotional service for a brief talk on meditation for beginners, the little crowd would be more than half composed of long-time meditators who just wanted to be in his presence. To the beginners he would say this: "Find a quiet place. Sit with the spine erect. Relax your body completely, your hands palm upward on your thighs, and your eyes gently focused on the point between the eyebrows - the Spiritual Eye, or Christ Consciousness Center. Begin with a prayer from your heart, with simple words, such as "Heavenly Father, Mother, Friend, Beloved God, saints of all religions, I bow to you all. Fill me with your love and bless my meditation."

"Then prepare the body by breathing in to a count of twenty, hold the breath for a count of twenty, and exhale for twenty. Do this at least six times. Then inhale twice quickly and tense the whole body, hold the tension to a count of three, and release the tension on a double exhalation. Do this several times. And then simply let the breath come as it will, without forcing, as if you were merely watching someone's else's breathing, with your eyes gently focused on the Spiritual Eye. When the breath comes in mentally chant "Love." While waiting and watching with detachment for the exhalation, focus your attention on the peace you begin to feel. When the breath wants to flow out, mentally chant "Peace," as you exhale."

"Thoughts will arise. Don't fight them. Just notice them, let them go, and return to your focus on the breath, the chant, and the growing peace."

Continue this for as long as you can, and then (he would tell us), exhale twice quickly and relax, focusing on the peace you feel. This peace is the first manifestation within you of the Beloved's Presence. In this peace, your communion can begin. Make it simple, he told us. Take a simple devotional phrase, one that touches your heart, and expresses your unique relationship to the Divine - a few simple words from the heart, such as, "I love you, Lord," or "Thou and I are one," or "Reveal Thyself," or "Fill me with Thy love." Or take the name of Divine Mother, and repeat your chosen words over and over again, with ever greater feeling, while concentrating at the heart. Imagine, he would say, that your heart itself has a mouth, and these words of love are being spoken by the heart itself, with ever deeper feeling, over and over again. If you feel no love as you repeat the words, then ask for love! Pray to feel more love, "teach me to love You. Fill me with Thy love."

Your yearning to feel love for your loving Source is itself the beginning of that love. Do not give up! Spirit has already begun to respond to you in subtle ways.

It may be that Spirit's response to you is present in this very moment now as you read these words, for the Beloved Herself lived in this saint, and now I share with you his words, not mine (and indeed his words were only those of our beloved guru, Yogananda). So these may therefore be divinely inspired words of guidance to you on how to draw closer to Spirit, in response to the longing for divine love that has brought you thus far in these pages.

(But you need not believe me or Brother Bhaktananda. Make the experiment and know for yourself!)

And then Brother would say, "Simply talk to God in the language of your heart, tell Him that you love Him, that you are seeking Him, that you want to know Him. Ask for His guidance in any troubles you may have, and pray for the well-being of those you love."

And then, like a doctor giving a prescription, he would say, "Ten to fifteen minutes in the morning, and again at night, and then for longer as you are able."

"Good night to you, and may Divine Mother bless you."

The Science of Love

There are deeper methods, and more powerful techniques to this loving science than the simple beginning that Brother Bhaktananda would share with us on Thursday nights. Each religious path has its version of this science: the whirling Sufis of Islam, the Kabbala of the Jews, among Christians the disciplines of the desert fathers or the ecstasies of devotional mystics such as St. Teresa of Avila. But it is in India that the science of meditation has been studied the longest, and to greatest depth, in an unbroken line of living spiritual culture stretching back five thousand years and more, where, amid a dazzling maze of paths to the Divine, the time-tested non-sectarian methods of yoga meditation emerged as India's great gift to humanity.

Practice of these methods need not compromise your faithfulness to your faith, your church, your mosque, your temple, your God. Remain true to your chosen Ideal, your image of the Beloved – and use, if you choose, these ways of yoga to discipline your body, your mind, your heart, your life-force itself to follow the inner road to blissful reunion with Spirit.

Christ said: "Love the Lord thy God with all thy mind, and all thy heart, and all thy soul, and all thy strength."

Doesn't this describe the depth and intensity of love your soul is craving? And the science of love, of yoga, is nothing more than a sure method whereby you may turn all your mind toward love, all your soul toward love, all your heart, and all your strength. That is, all your life-force, all your consciousness, all your concentration, focused into a laser-like beam of adoration which can burn through the veils that separate you from the One who loves you.

It is, in truth, an art and science of making love to God.

When we use this phrase to refer to the "tender indignities of physical love," it may be easy to lose sight of the higher reality of which the act of union is often only a sweet but fleeting reminder.

And yet, when we speak of "making love" to the Divine, the words are touchingly apt, for the reality is nothing less than a merging of essence, an offering up, in a surrender both yearning and urgent, of one's whole being, body and soul, to the One you love. The sweetness, the passion, the high joy of this union are the surpassing reality behind every love song ever composed.

And if you would offer your whole being, you must learn to control it. That is what yoga meditation is.

It is possible to achieve a deeply romantic and fulfilling relationship with the Beloved without these methods. But if you would dispense with them, then you must have a devotional gift of great intensity, because the inner path is the same no matter what the method, and to merge your being with God by virtue only of your own loving will is a daunting task. Every religion can boast of great souls who have reached the Beloved armed only with intensity of yearning. But almost always, they were monks, priests, nuns or rabbis, often hidden away in monasteries and ashrams, living lives of celibacy and solitude.

For us, the lovers who linger in the busy world and who yet yearn for God, the help of this science of love can be indispensable.

Finding the Method

The world has ten thousand seductions ready to hand, all of them gifts from the One handed out to see if you still prefer the gifts to the Giver. You wouldn't be reading this book if these gifts were enough for you! You would be out agonizing over a heartbreaking love-affair, or briefly triumphing in the achievement of a worldly goal, or wondering why the achievement of that goal (accomplished in the long-ago of only last year) has left you discontented, or resenting the success of those less deserving than you, or engaged in any of the trillion pursuits with which you have whiled away the eons, while your Lover waits for you.

But now you are seeking the Lover. And since the whole cosmos is only a titanic game of Love, be sure that She won't let the game end suddenly or easily, merely because you've begun to wonder if She's real. Your yearning will drive you, and She will test you.

CHAPTER 15

▲ ▲ ▲

Meddling in the Occult

To tell the whole story of how I very nearly lost both soul and life through meddling in the occult may someday be another book. For now, I will tell you that to open oneself to trance-channeling, psychic phenomena, and amateur hypnosis is to invite what my Guru called "tramp souls" into your mind and physical vehicle. In my case, a woman opened herself to such low-level discarnate entities as a means of fascinating me. The course of such an action is fairly predictable. Souls who linger on the earth plane after death are usually unevolved beings tied here by yearning for the physical pleasures of the body. When one foolishly invites them in, they will tell you whatever they think you want to hear, so as to keep the game going. Appeals to one's ego, tales of heroic past lives, hints of prophetic powers, will reliably emerge to keep the channel open. This can lead to mental disease.

And sometimes fairly dark things may ensue. Threats on my life were spoken by such an entity, and my younger sister (who knew nothing of my experiments) had nightmares about an evil force in my bedroom. Two days later the entity seemed to make good on its threat, and I came close to dying in a strange fire. Had I slept a quarter of an hour longer that morning, it is unlikely that you would be reading this page.

But worse was the spiritual damage. I became swept up in what Carl Jung called "inflation" — in which a mythic and archetypal dynamic is mistaken for an individual reality, in which the Hero's Journey becomes, not a purifying quest for realization, but a deluded ego trip for vain glory. It is common in such cases to hear whispers of a great purpose and destiny, and to imagine that one has been born with a great work to do.

Romancing the Divine

As Brother Bhaktananda would later tell me, this is quite true. Each of us has indeed been born with a great and heroic work to do – the liberation of our own soul from delusory identification with the body, and the blissful reunion with our Loving Source – a quest every bit as glorious and perilous as that of Galahad or Perseus. But it is all too easy to look for a more glamorous and less humble version of this heroic work, some more exciting and grandiose alternative to the long haul of spiritual development.

In a heady three-year trajectory of psychic phenomena, sexual initiation, and career recognition that landed me finally in America's most exalted palace of the arts, my ego was given every reason to believe that, in my case, "inflation" was merely the truth.

But the psychic phenomena would turn out to be insidious snares, the sexual initiation would become emotional enmeshment, and the exalted palace would turn out to be a temple to a god I no longer worshipped.

Recovery from this damage took a long time. It would be years before my search for God became sufficiently grounded to draw an illumined teacher.

And the woman who invited these entities into her mind descended into obsession, and suffered serious mental and physical damage, for which I may bear some blame. I may excuse myself that I was nineteen, and she was fifteen years my senior, and in the position of a mentor. But the unattractive truth is that I was fascinated, and pursued this perilous path because it fed my ego.

To be sure, there was plenty of sensational evidence to convince me that genuine past-life material was in play, that some authentic level of information was being accessed. Entities will happily provide such parlor tricks as long as you keep providing a warm body for them to temporarily inhabit. Psychic powers are realities - the phenomena is well-documented. However, they not only have no bearing on authentic spirituality, they are a positive hindrance and danger.

CHAPTER 16

Discipline

PERHAPS IT ALL sounds too easy. Love the Lover. Find a method. Practice the Presence. Float into bliss.

Yet this romance is an art as well as a science, and so — as with any art worthy of the name — there is a discipline to be mastered.

Now I have the joy of sharing with you perhaps the most encouraging reality at my disposal. Believe me when I tell you that if I can feel Her presence, if I can tell you from my heart and on my soul that She is real, if I can speak from personal experience (from the little meditation I have done, and from the faltering but dogged efforts I have made) and can assure you that God will walk with you and tangibly hold your hand — if one like me can promise you that His Light in meditation is real — then trust me on this: if I can get this far, then anyone who longs for closeness with the Divine surely can too.

Fulsome carryings on about one's imperfections are tedious, so I will not weary you with them. Suffice it to say that discipline is not exactly my middle name, that I have often been reduced to slack-jawed amazement that one who has strayed as blithely as I have should also be so abundantly blessed, that I have often thought to myself that Divine Mother nowhere proves Her compassion more conclusively than in Her sweet condescension to my dubious charms.

My saving grace is that I want very badly to love Her in reality, and that I have never let my failings keep me from reaching for Her hand. Simply put, I will never give up.

Romancing the Divine

The testimony and guidance of those great ones who have reached the heights of union is an indispensable blessing. I am only here because such a one came back for me. Do not accept this book as a substitute for such guidance! The testimony of such a soul does not consist of mere words – he or she can be a channel for Divinity itself, and can open the door to ecstasy for those whose souls are ready.

But I felt prompted to offer you these words because I sensed that the testimony of one who has been dragged by doggedness and lifted by grace to a place not even half-way up the mountain may also be of help.

I will tell you later on of Brother Turiyananda – Divine Mother's bad boy – an ardent devotee whose stumbles were as inspiring to us, in some ways, as the blessedness of others; an impassioned lover who stormed his way to God by sheer desire and tenderness, who overcame bleak depression and wayward habits to die with a smile of perfect bliss on his face. Stories of Turiyananda have kept many of us on the path over the years - have seduced us into believing that if we cling fiercely to Her hand despite our failings, as he did, then this may just be enough to lift us into Love.

But Turiyananda had a will of iron as well as a heart of gold, and there are hard facts to the science of this love. If over time you do not work to develop devotional habits, and take time each day to go within, then this book may merely join other inspiring tales on your shelf that point the way to paths you never explored.

And for my part, if I do not open my heart to you at this essential moment, and tell you in candor of the necessity of discipline, and of my struggles toward it, then you may someday rightly suspect me of spinning a glib seduction with only the ignoble aim of obtaining an author's share of the price of this book.

For the truth is that I had to make hard sacrifices, take great risks, and go on a long journey to finally instill devotional discipline in my life - and the struggle still goes on.

Michael Henry Dunn

But it is a sweet struggle now, for the Lover is with me - as She always was, of course - and now as I swim upstream against the current, I am a fish firmly impaled on Her loving hook, and now it is just a tender sport between us when I resist Her homeward pull.

Remember, however, that it may not be such a struggle for you, as I was a hard case. For there were seven years of desultory efforts and frustrated longing after I opened the Dwarf's Door before I committed in earnest. Being an artist can be as much a malady as a gift, and we are often only as disciplined as our self-expression requires. I saw plainly near the end of those years that, as my teacher said, "environment is stronger than will" - especially if the will was mine!

Your environment may not need the radical shift that mine required. Three and a half years of chopping onions and mopping floors in a monastery kitchen are not a prerequisite to feeling the presence of the Beloved!

Nearly twenty years have passed since then, and as I look back now, I see that it was the simple things that kept me close to Her. Reaching for Her hand. Seeing Her in the sunlight and in the light of human eyes. A tender inner conversation. Chanting the Name within throughout the day. And meditation.

Meditation. There is no substitute for it. The Lover is within. The world draws us out. Meditation opens the inner door and shuts out the world for a time, so that we may commune with the Beloved in the silence, and experience the reality of the soul as peace, as joy, and emerge refreshed again for the joyous battle of life.

Without some form of meditative practice, you may yearn to be a divine lover, and yet remain the world's fool.

In India I sat down under a tree with a few other souls one fine morning to talk with a monk about God. When the talk turned to meditation, a blissful smile stole over his face, and he closed his eyes, and whispered a single word several times over with tender reverence. It was not a name of God. It was not a holy phrase. It was rather, he said, the key to bliss.

"Ahh!" he murmured dreamily, "Regularity in meditation! Regularity! Regularity!"

However, he was, be it remembered, a monk! Celibate. Cloistered. No rent to pay. No children to raise. No boss to please or business to run. No mortgage. No commute. Immune from global recession and world upheaval, living a life of service and simplicity that he had earned and chosen as a young man.

So let us not judge ourselves by monastic standards! Begin simply. Take even fifteen minutes in the morning (or five, or ten, but begin!), and again before bed to meditate and pray, and once a week for an hour or longer, and your life will begin to change. Practice your Beloved's presence. Chant the Name in silence whenever you can, and see the One in all. Forgive yourself quickly for neglect or distraction in your practice, renounce the great temptation of self-condemnation, and merely keep on keeping on. Do this, and He will become real to you. You will know Him, in time, as your true and unfailing Lover and Friend.

CHAPTER 17

▲▲▲

The Pendant

SHE WAS A brilliant director in the theater, a master manipulator of her actors, intuitively able to either hold up a mirror to the best in them, or to play on their vulnerabilities - always to the greater supposed good of the production, of course. Of blended Polish-Gypsy-Jewish descent, she possessed a powerful magnetism, but lacked the emotional maturity to use it well. An award-winning stage actress who had studied at the famed Pasadena Playhouse, Zosh was not conventionally attractive, but was compelling nonetheless. She was thirty-five, a divorced mother of two. I was nineteen.

She died nearly twenty years ago now, and by the time she passed I had prayed intensely that her soul would heal – and that I would never encounter her again.

I recognized the potential dangers of the relationship early on, and had withdrawn from it. But the weird workings of karma took a hand, and we were cast in absurdly accurate archetypal roles in the Chicago premiere of Leonard Bernstein's "Candide" – she played The Gypsy Woman, and I played the titular sunny and innocent incarnation of naiveté. The production was a highly anticipated one and its success put a heady spin on the emerging affair.

On the opening night, Zosh revealed to me her previously hidden worldview, and gave me a powerful talisman – which in the years to come would become an instrument of manipulation.

Romancing the Divine

Over candlelight and Black Russians in her living room in a three-bedroom bungalow in a Chicago suburb, she took out a solid-gold pendant on a chain. Within a circlet, a delicately sculpted man's hand and a woman's hand (also of gold) were intertwined, holding up goblets in a toast, with pearls embedded in each goblet. Around the rim was spelled out in several languages words of toasting – *"Salud" "Ein Prosit" "Cheers" "L'Chaim."* And on the back a personalized engraving from the original gift-giver who had ordered the piece. There Darryl Zanuck, legendary movie mogul, had inscribed the words, "for six months of outstanding performances," in recognition of the work of 1940's film star Linda Darnell. Named by Look magazine as "One of the Four Most Beautiful Women in the World," Darnell had once been among the elite stars of Hollywood.

On this night, with great solemnity Zosh told me that Darnell had given her the pendant in recognition of a deep spiritual connection between them, shortly before she was killed in a fire. And now, it seemed, the spirit of Darnell had come to Zosh in meditation, and instructed her to give the pendant to me as a symbol of my membership in this unnamed mystic kinship. An unspoken implication that night was that "Candide" was to follow the spiritual guidance of "The Gypsy," if he was to achieve his spiritual destiny.

Zosh intoned unrecognizable words in some presumably intergalactic tongue in my ears, and handed me the pendant.

Words of protective conditioning came back to me from my Mind Control training, "I can accept or reject whatever is offered me, at this or any other level of the mind."

I took the pendant. I was dimly aware that I was also accepting a powerfully charged manipulative device, but the object itself was beautiful and precious, the affair (at that point) was intensely entertaining, and my career was taking off. A talisman given by a legendary mogul to a tragic movie star proved irresistible. The idea of my membership in some mystic brotherhood was titillating, but I experienced no inner confirmation. Though I was merely nineteen,

Michael Henry Dunn

I somehow intuited that a sticky ego trap was being laid for me, but believed I could dance through it and around it.

After a brief stint in college that fall, I returned to Chicago to pursue my acting career, and the fascination deepened. A lighthearted indulgence with the Ouija Board led to Zosh going into trance, and the box of mischief sprung open wide.

The emerging trance narrative went something like this: We were both members of some ancient mystical order, had come to the planet with an age-long mission of upliftment of the race, but were subject to errors and temptations. That the trance sessions themselves were rife with error and temptation was not yet apparent to me, nor that my acceptance of the pendant given by Linda Darnell to Zosh shortly before her death by fire would presage my own narrow escape from the same fate.

CHAPTER 18

▲▲▲

The Fire

"You must prepare. You will be given a place, and books, and time."

So said a being who called herself "Fara" (an entity channeled through Zosh) who may or may not have been from another dimension, who may or may not have been a split-off pathological projection of a repressed aspect of Zosh herself, but who (this one time at any rate) was impressively accurate in her prediction.

My parents had just finished an extensive remodeling of our home with the intention of putting it on the market — had even gone so far as to buy a slightly smaller house in the neighboring suburb of River Forest — and all was in readiness. My boyhood home was soon to be sold.

On that day, I slept long and uneasily in the smallest bedroom, in the far corner of the third floor next to the room we had called "The Chapel" (the house once having been owned by a religious order). The relationship with Zosh, which had begun in shared artistic enthusiasm and mutual fascination, had begun to show signs of the obsession that would eventually destroy it (my teenage training in control of my own mind protected me, I now believe, from worse damage, but at that time I was still in the thrall of the sensational material). My youngest sister Julie, who doted on me as I did on her, had experienced a nightmare the previous night about an evil figure in my room, who said to her, "This room is death." That week, a hostile entity calling itself "Tanta" (who claimed to hold a lethal grudge against me for some ancient past-life offense) had achieved what appeared to be complete control of Zosh's body for a time, and had reached out to the chain of the pendant around my neck, and began to slowly draw it in a choking circlet around my throat. Alarmed, I had managed to bring Zosh back, but feared we had stirred up something over which we were losing control.

On that day I dozed and tossed the morning away, and then received a distracted call from Zosh. She sounded strange and emotionally fraught. She insisted that I meet her at noon. I reluctantly promised, but was gripped by an odd languor, and lingered in bed.

My father was headed to the airport to fly to San Diego. My mother, also about to leave, called up the stairs that someone would have to remain home to open the door for the electrician. I was tempted to volunteer, to ignore Zosh's growing strangeness, and to sleep on, but at the last minute I jumped from bed, and left my brother Chris to answer the door.

If not for this last minute decision, I would have been alone in the house, asleep in my bed when the gas-powered drier exploded a few minutes later in the laundry room beneath me.

Instead, oblivious to the fact that my home was in flames, I drove to meet Zosh at the studio where she taught acting.

I was shocked at the sight of her face. A bleak pallor and barely restrained rage showed in her features. She looked ill and weak.

More shock was to come. She had suffered a miscarriage, she told me, of a pregnancy she had known of for some weeks, but had hidden from me. Her plan had been to arrange for me to go away to some school, and to bear the child without my knowledge. It was to be a "special child" – but now she knew she was not the "chosen vessel," and she was consumed by bitterness and loss.

Anger swept over me at this twisted manipulative scheme whereby a life-long claim on me had been created without my knowledge or consent, from which I had only narrowly escaped. My anger was tempered by compassion for her ordeal, but now I knew beyond doubt that I was in a dangerous relationship, that a grandiosely inflated fantasy was being foisted on me, in which my genuine spiritual yearnings were being gradually smothered.

I drove home shaken and sobered. Coming up the leafy tunnel of the street I grew up on, I passed fire trucks coming the other way. At home, the third shock of the morning awaited — blackened smoking heaps of rubble lay on the lawn of my home, and the second floor was scarred by charred streaks, shattered windows, and whisps of lingering smoke. I leaped from the car, fearing for my family.

"No one was hurt," a fireman assured me. The dryer beneath my room had exploded, my brother Chris had barely escaped with his life, and the house had been severely damaged. Had I been at home, asleep above the explosion, it is doubtful I would have lived.

The rest of my family moved into the newly purchased home in River Forest, while our old home was repaired. Eventually we would move back into it to stay. For a while, I stayed as caretaker in the fire-scarred home, walking up three flights in the darkness and the pervasive smell of smoke to sleep alone in one of the undamaged rooms.

And then a neighbor offered her home for the summer. A widowed bookstore proprietor, she would be away in Canada for six months, and needed a caretaker. I moved into a six-bedroom mansion that had been remodeled by Frank Lloyd Wright — wherein the late Victorian décor and bric-a-brac appeared not to have been altered since 1910. Light played down through the banisters into the halls, and I found myself ensconced in the master suite that had belonged to her late husband, a Protestant minister. It was filled with books on philosophy and religion.

"You will be given a place, and books, and time," the channel had said. "To prepare. "

But for what?

CHAPTER 19

▲▲▲

Escape from Monkey Island

THERE ARE TIMES, I have found, when the Goddess has had no choice but to intervene directly in my life — when I have blundered down the wrong path with such conviction that I unwittingly force her hand. She does this so deftly that it is usually only in retrospect that I see it. In later years, when she appeared to me in a canyon after I called her name in terror, it took some hours for the miracle to dawn on me — at the time it all seemed normal. Perhaps someday she may come to me in spectacular glory, but it seems plain I haven't earned that yet, though I dream of it. In the canyon, when I thought I might be about to die, it was enough that I called her and she appeared. Most often, she chooses to work in secret.

It's not that we don't have free will, and it's not as if we are relieved entirely of the consequences of our errors, but there's this thing called Grace.

In the story I share now, she took so many threads of my life into her hand at once — in a single week — weaving a pattern of future consequences so powerful that I still look back in awe at the sequence of it. And I laugh, too, as the story contains much that is absurd.

I had turned twenty-one and had taken the wrong path. Wrong in the sense that my soul's purpose was now thoroughly thwarted, while the charm of the sensational had not yet worn thin. I had caught Zosh's disease, so to speak, and saw grandiose destiny at every turn. In the aftermath of the fire, as I settled into my splendid isolation in the minister's library, I began to see that in fact I had no path, no guide, and no concept by which to

Romancing the Divine

approach the Source. Zosh seemed to want psychic fireworks, and an escape into the fantasy of reincarnational myth-making. I would suspect later that she was addicted to romance – but to a false shallow romance, not the passionate inner path to Reality I would come to know in later years, but to a movie-land fantasy, to romance as escape from life's relentless demand for growth.

I knew at least enough to understand that I was merely a callow youth with no inter-galactic message to pronounce to the less-evolved. But I could not yet see that I was in thrall to a dangerous delusion foisted on me by a woman of much magnetism and little maturity. I had allowed myself to play with fire, complacent that I could avoid spiritual damage, and had almost literally been burned.

But this much at least was authentic in me: I wanted to know God, and I wanted to be of service.

The late minister whose suite I now occupied had wide-ranging taste in reading: thick theological tomes by Hans Küng, a dozen different Bibles (including, to my awe, one printed in 1587 by the printer to Her Majesty, Queen Elizabeth the First), a number of works on "the historical Jesus," and one book in particular that caught my eye – "A New Synthesis of Evolution," a distillation of the thought of French paleontologist and Jesuit priest, Pierre Teilhard de Chardin. Here was an accomplished scientist, yet a Catholic steeped in loyalty to Mother Church, who had been silenced by the Vatican for articulating a revolutionary vision of an upward-spiraling interwoven ascent of Spirit and Matter, crowned in the Christ-potential of the "phenomenon of Man."

For the first time, my questing mind glimpsed a path of reconciliation with my yearning heart. It would be years before they were truly joined. In the meantime, I was an ambitious young actor who was finally allowing himself to know that he could be as good as he dreamed of being.

Michael Henry Dunn

That summer I worked as a tele-charge operator at The Shubert Theater in Chicago's Loop, selling tickets to the Broadway tours that came through town. Then I would take the El train back to my private mansion in Oak Park, and retreat into the stuffy time machine of 1910 Victoriana and liberal Protestant theology, amid Frank Lloyd Wright's elegant play of light and fine wood. But Hans Küng was not for me – I soaked up Teilhard, and studied the life and works of Gandhi. I decided to fast on water for three days – with no clear purpose other than that it was extolled by Gandhi as a purifying thing. My dreams were deeper, my step lighter, and my mind clearer. I began to chafe at the dominating influence of Zosh, whose mystic detachment as a supposed spiritual guide had proven to be heavily diluted with self-seeking and emotional insecurity.

Meantime, my career began to blossom with exciting and challenging work, lead roles, and recognition. I wanted to be an actor with a capital "A" – to receive classical training, to emulate my idol, Laurence Olivier, and reinterpret the great Shakespearean roles. My first acquaintance with Zosh had been when I sought her out as an acting coach on a friend's recommendation to help me prepare my audition for the finest classical academy in the country – The Juilliard School at New York City's glittering palace of performing art, Lincoln Center. Through one of those "accidents" of fate, my audition time was mishandled by the school, and I was denied my chance, remaining in Chicago to further my career.

Still all that while, I sensed that the theater, much as I loved it, would not satisfy me, that some authentic path was waiting only brief years away – one which would lead beyond the joy of performing to something I longed for more deeply, which I could not really name or describe.

But first the Goddess had to rescue me from the trap, remove Zosh from my life, get me out of Chicago, and introduce me to the woman who would become my wife.

I was not cooperating.

Romancing the Divine

It was Christmas. Our burned-out home had been restored, and we had moved back in, where I now had something like a private apartment in the basement. I was finishing up a run of Dickens' classic "A Christmas Carol" at The Goodman Theater – Chicago's premiere venue at that time. I had auditioned at another prominent Chicago theater, The Body Politic, for the lead in Frank Wedekind's German tale of angst-ridden youth, "Spring's Awakening," and had been called back several times for further auditions. This would be a breakthrough. A lead role, a prominent theater, my union card, and an artistic challenge. "Give us three days," the director told me. "If we don't call you back by that time, we've given the role to someone else."

I had by this time developed the thick skin necessary to survive as an actor. When the call didn't come after three days, I chalked it up, and was ready to move on.

It was the night of the final performance at the Goodman. I came home to find my brothers Peter and Mark gathered with two friends in the kitchen, hatching a plan to fly to Puerto Rico the next morning for $50 round trip. Extra seats were available on a charter flight through a friend's connections. We would escape Chicago's brutal winter for a week-long sunny adventure in the tropics. We knew no one in Puerto Rico, had no hotel reservations, and very little money. Flush out of cash (as I often was), I borrowed $200 from my friend Lane (who would accompany us), and agreed to join them.

We thought it prudent not to mention our plans to our parents until we called from O'Hare airport, just before boarding. My father was appalled.

"You don't just *go* to Puerto Rico!"

But go we did.

Now I should mention here that I had received a chain letter two days before. The kind that promises you unexpected good fortune if you send it on, and threatens malefic consequences if you break the chain, that cites woeful tales of those who dared to neglect their luck, and of the amazing grace that came to those who sent the blessing forward.

I'd had my fill of superstition at that point, but I couldn't quite bring myself to just throw the letter out. I put it in my pocket, and forgot about it.

We suffered through a miserable first night in a frog-infested campground before we found an idyllic vacation center at Punta Santiago, on the east coast of the island. For scant dollars per night, we each had a bunk in an airy cabin mere feet from the beach, a sturdy little kitchen, and quick help from some local teens (Edwin Dalvela was his name, I think – a fifteen-year-old father of two), who brought out long nets whereby we feasted on fresh crab, drank Ronrico rum, and composed whimsical tunes on my guitar. Several days of perfect adventure followed, until it occurred to me that it would be considerate at that point to call my parents, to let them know we were doing just fine. I found a phone booth, and dared to call collect.

My mother's voice was chilly with condemnation. And then she dropped the bombshell. One hour after our plane took off for Puerto Rico, the director had called to offer me the lead at The Body Politic. But for the only time in my entire life, my parents had no way of getting in touch with me. In those days before cell phones, before the Internet, they knew only that I was somewhere on the island of Puerto Rico. The director needed a commitment, and he gave the part to someone else.

I was stunned. The chain letter's curse had struck. To lose such a chance for a reason so trivial! It brought to mind the famous scene from "Patton," wherein the great George C. Scott as the quixotic general fumes that he is being denied his destiny for merely slapping a soldier. "God will not permit this to happen! This has to be the will of God!"

Romancing the Divine

I told my brother Mark the appalling news. He gave scant comfort. "Well, Michael," he said, "there are two kinds of actors in the world. There are those who go on to become famous stars. And there are those who go to Puerto Rico."

We were, be it remembered, of Irish heritage. This kind of caustic remark is what still passes for filial love among our tribe.

"No!" I insisted. "God must have had some great and overriding purpose to take me two thousand miles from home, and drop me on this island, incommunicado with Mom and Dad for the only seven-day period in my whole life – just so I would not take that part!"

I walked down the beach alone, trying to shake off the gloom of the thing. The beaches there were not idyllic: trash-strewn, littered with broken-down beach houses, sprinkled with dog droppings. I kept my face toward the ocean, reached in my pocket – and found the chain letter.

An empty bottle of Ronrico rum lay in the sand. I unscrewed the cap, inserted the letter, fastened it tightly, walked out on a long pier, and cast it eastward into the surf towards the coast of Africa, three thousand miles away. Some poor West African will find it, I thought, and I only hope he doesn't decide on a whim to fly to Puerto Rico and so lose the girl of his dreams while he's out of town.

Feeling lighter, as if I had released the curse, I returned to my brothers.

The next day would be our last before the flight home. As we cast our nets for crab that week, a small palmy island had beckoned from what seemed like a short distance off shore. "Come explore me, brave boys!" it sang. We were told its name was the Island of the Monkeys. Were there monkeys there, we asked? Nobody knew, as our local friends had never bothered to go.

Michael Henry Dunn

"Let's swim to the island!" said Lane. I did not take him seriously – he was prone to eccentric notions. But now on this last morning, there he was, strapping on his flippers, and encouraging my brothers to join him. To my disbelief, they were actually wading into the surf, none of them in great shape, intent on swimming to an island I was sure must be at least five times further than it looked, through waters that were likely feeding grounds for sharks, for no other purpose than a lark.

I furiously shouted at them to come back, but they ignored me, and so I had no choice. I waded in, and we began what would be a fateful swim.

The island was indeed much further than it seemed. The flippers were an additional absurdity – weighing down our feet, and providing little extra propulsion. Our arms grew more leaden with each stroke, more salt water spilled down our throats, and the island came no closer as an hour crawled by. The foolhardiness of the thing was now fully upon us, but we convinced ourselves we were past the halfway point, and that we could rest on the Island of the Monkeys.

At last, as our reserves of strength ebbed, we came in close sight of the beach. We felt the rocks beneath our feet – sharp rocks that cut the skin, sending just the number of parts per million of blood into the sea needed to alert the exquisitely attuned sensors of lurking sharks. We staggered towards the shore, desperate for rest.

And then we saw why none of our newfound local friends had ever set foot on Monkey Island.

Stark signs in government-issue stenciled capital font, black letters on white background, were thrust into the sand at regular intervals:

"KEEP OUT! DANGER! U.S. GOVERNMENT QUARANTINE! NO TRESPASSING! DANGER! QUARANTINE!"

Romancing the Divine

This gave us pause. This was frightening. But we had no choice. We could not go back into the surf in our exhausted condition, where we would drown, or draw sharks. Tentatively, we staggered onto the beach. I watched Lane disappear behind a shrub, where he sought to relieve nature. A moment later I saw him back out of the shrub, a picture of shock, unable to say anything but, "Oh my God, oh my God, oh my God!"

Following him out of the shrub was an enormous, full-grown male ape of indeterminate species, unrestrained, uncaged, and very wild.

Ah, yes. The Island of the Monkeys.

We barely had time to scream, or shout, or grab a stick to defend ourselves. A moment later, a khaki-clad woman with a pistol on her hip and rage on her face strode out from the bush, and began to scream and swear at us. "Get off this island! Now! Get back in that water! Leave! Now!"

We tried to plead our case, but she was in some kind of panic and would not hear a word. "Off this island! Now! Right now! Are you out of your minds?"

Her hand was on her gun. We staggered back into the surf, inflicting more cuts on our unprotected feet, and stood helplessly chest-deep in water, afraid to go in, and unable to go back.

What the quarantine was for, why the apes were roaming free, what experiments the U.S. government was conducting, or what disease it was attempting to control, we would never learn.

When the Goddess places you, for reasons of Her own, in a perilous situation, it is my experience that She will provide help when asked for. And even my atheistical friend Lane had been invoking divine aid with fervor, as we faced the long swim back.

Michael Henry Dunn

And so a small fishing boat approached, little more than a rowboat with a motor tacked on, steered by a chubby Puerto Rican wielding a harpoon gun.

We waved feebly. He got the picture, and waved back. We climbed aboard, and told our tale. He was aghast. "You swam! You swam to the Island of the Monkeys! I never do that, man! Sharks! Barracuda! You are lucky I'm here!"

Yes, I suppose we'll call it luck.

And so we returned safely to Chicago, just as the second-worst blizzard of the century pounded the city. And then the flip side of the chain letter kicked in – like the legends on the letter itself telling of how the evil fate was reversed when the letter was sent on – the blessings were triggered as the bottle of rum floated east with the tides toward Africa. The next day, I auditioned at an up-and-coming theater called the St. Nicholas for an original musical – a quirky piece about a disabled songwriter called "Funeral March for a One-Man Band." I was cast in a lead role. I won my union card. The play was a smash hit. I received the city's acting award. The director got me into The Juilliard School, and I left for New York the following autumn, leaving the toxic influence of Zosh behind as I landed unexpectedly in the exalted palace of the arts of which I had dreamed. In that cast at St. Nicholas, I met Alicia (I will confess that she played my mother), my future wife, whose innate and grounded spirituality would help me recover my true bearings when I returned from New York to revive the play three years later.

And Zosh fell ill with a strange fainting sickness that no one could diagnose, identified only as "an unknown tropical crystal," that she must have picked up from some one who had been to the Caribbean. She lost her job in the national touring company of "Annie" because of this fainting malady – and so some few months later she was free to be cast in a new comedy on Broadway, following me to New York a year later, where the obsession at last became starkly obvious, and I cut the tie.

Romancing the Divine

She would follow me back to Chicago, too, and afterwards a decade later to Los Angeles, and the obsessive silent phone calls in the middle of the night, after my marriage, with only the sound of breathing – those would come to an end only years later. The medallion I had given back long before, grateful to be rid of the glittering tool of seduction, with the sad karma of Linda Darnell still clinging to it.

And when Zosh came to Los Angeles to work in film, where I was safely in the service of my guru, cooking meals for monks, she would write one last letter to pull me back in, and I would be tempted to reach out in friendship to see if she had healed. And Brother Bhaktananda would then give me the only piece of direct and blunt advice I would ever receive from him, when I asked in a counseling session if I should call her.

With all the quiet power of his bliss, he looked directly into my eyes:

"No contact," he said. "No contact."

The Goddess had worked very hard to bring me home, and Brother was taking no chances.

But closure was given, nevertheless. A chance encounter with a Chicago actor, two years later, brought me the news that Zosh had brain cancer, with only weeks to live. And so I called to say good-bye. It is twenty years ago now.

She haunts me playfully now and again – most often at movie theaters....she always wanted life to be like the movies. I acknowledge her presence, kid her about bothering me still, and let her go.

CHAPTER 20

The Glittering Palace

(Student days at The Juilliard School – Photo by Peter Lane at the Temple of Dendur in the Metropolitan Museum of Art)

"You are the aristocracy of talent."

So said Peter Mennin, president of The Juilliard School, to the assembled first year students of all three divisions of the famed academy – Music, Drama, and Dance. He then briskly reminded us that talent alone would not suffice if we were to fulfill our potential. Still, I thought it likely, as I walked out of Alice Tully Hall that morning, that most of the young artists there were saying to themselves, "Wow! I'm the aristocracy of talent!"

Romancing the Divine

The egos assembled in that hall were not what you'd call paltry, and mine was rather more inflated than most at that point. For though I had escaped the psychic snares, and though I had a genuine longing for God and to be of service, the trajectory of events that had landed me in the gorgeous cultural palace of Lincoln Center had persuaded me that some powerful destiny was at work, and that the world would soon be at my feet…whereupon (I told myself) I would leave it to find God.

However, as Peter Mennin could have told me (and probably did), the secret ingredient that must be blended with talent to achieve success in the fiercely competitive world of Manhattan is one-pointed determination fueled by intensity of desire. To already be looking past the discipline one had come to the academy to acquire was a guarantee of failure, as I would soon discover.

It is true that I would wander through Central Park in my free time rehearsing Shakespearean soliloquies. But it is also true that I would rhythmically repeat phrases from the Our Father as I walked to Lincoln Center from my apartment in Times Square. It is true that attending Broadway openings (with multiple celebrities in attendance) was thrilling. It is also true that I spent a fair amount of time alone at St. Malachy's Church just off 8th Avenue.

I read Huxley's mystical commentaries. I read The Bhaghavad Gita. I read The Cloud of Unknowing. I had a dream one morning of which I remembered only the phrase "Tertium Organum" – and "happened upon" the esoteric metaphysical work of that name by Gurdjieff in a bookstore that afternoon. I began to see that to truly know God would be a long hard haul, would require discipline, would require a teacher, a path, a community. But I was still caught in the web of my own karma, and could not simply (as J.D. Salinger put it) "walk out on the results of my own hankerings." But neither did I have the heart any longer for the savagely focused ambition needed to make it in New York.

Michael Henry Dunn

After two years, I saw that the classical polish and top-level contacts that I had come to New York to acquire came at a spiritual price I was not willing to pay. My decision to leave Juilliard before graduation cost me the contacts...and my parents' support for a time as well. In light of normal and sensible career considerations, my action was that of an arrogant, headstrong, and spiritually bewildered young man. The heady trajectory of destiny that had seemed to guide my path had vanished, and I learned what it was to go hungry, to be lonely, to be merely one of the faceless ambitious thousands dwarfed by the cold inhuman scale of Midtown. Even my love of the theater seemed to atrophy, and my talent seemed to go weak. After leaving Juilliard, I worked as a short-order cook for a time – my ticket (if only I had known it) to eventual employment preparing meals for the monks in the peaceful lakeside monastery that would become, a decade later, my spiritual home.

But now we have circled back to where we started. I returned to Chicago, where God would break open my heart, and give me a brief taste of Her bliss.

CHAPTER 21

▲▲▲

Marriage and Meditation

I FIND MYSELF reluctant to share with you the story of my two marriages. But that is just the ego wanting to paint the handsomer picture, to daub the harder edges with strokes of vagueness, and to make my journey seem easier and more attractive, and myself a more likable fellow. As ever, the truth is more useful, and as I unabashedly desire to win hearts for Her if I can, and since I write this for those who, like me, cannot help wanting it all – human love in all its warmth and comfort, divine love in all its fullness and completion – I will share with you briefly my stumbles, lessons, and blessings on the path of marriage.

For here in this moment of reluctance to reveal myself, I remember how the story ends, and I brighten up. The hard-won knowledge that what you think of me is of little importance, the growing awareness that in any case this name and this body are nothing more than a fleeting moth-light fading into Her loving darkness, and the sense that these pages are a gift of gratitude to Her and only secondarily (perhaps) a chance for Her to draw you closer....these realizations make it easier for me to tell my unvarnished truth.

And as a storyteller, I remember that I have worthwhile tales to tell, and that my life is blessed beyond my dreams, and so I will not skip over anything worth telling.

So let us keep the story unfolding in its true order. We have circled back to our starting point – the slowly healing heart, the shattered soul-mate dream, and the beckoning monastery. When I opened the Dwarf's Door, I had returned from New York, had just turned twenty-five, and was enduring one of those periodic dry spells that are the lot of ninety-nine percent of the actors in the world. My thirst for communion with Source had become unignorable and a path suddenly seemed to open with the little book I'd found. But, of course, one last golden illusory "big break" beckoned that might keep me tied to the theater. If that door should close, I told myself, I would take it as a sign that the God I wanted to love waited for me in the monastery.

But the door stayed open. The director from New York cast me after all. I did not make the journey to meet the Trappist abbot in Iowa. And I met again the woman we will call Alicia.

Voices have always mattered to me. The timbre, the tone, the dulcet hints in the lower range, the "listenability" of a voice – these have always exerted a hypnotic pull. So as I sat in a car on Chicago's North Side, car-pooling back from a friend's opening with a couple other actors, Alicia's warm, incisive and ironic tones seemed to echo in some unfilled chamber in my mind and heart that I couldn't quite identify.

She was eleven years my senior. She was a seasoned actress who seemed to never stop working. She was the adult child of a recovering alcoholic whose journey through the Twelve Steps would open my eyes to the reality of addiction. Like me, she was a "recovering Catholic" – but one with a stronger antipathy to the church – for that matter, to *any* church. And she would turn out to be an extraordinarily gifted therapist and spiritual leader, as our marriage would become a journey towards a more radically different life and work for both than either foresaw.

Environment, my Master observed, is stronger than will. So in choosing a mate, you are choosing an environment – one that can be a garden of growth, or a stagnant by-water. And it is a sad and unavoidable truth of marriage that it can start out as the one and end as the other.

Marriage as a Trap, Marriage as a Path

In India they are much more realistic about marriage than we in the West. They expect much less of it, and so often receive much more. In India they do not suffer from the romantic expectations that marriage was saddled with in the West – the "knight in shining armor finds his princess" heritage of medieval romances, embedded into our culture during the Renaissance by that pesky fellow Shakespeare and his Juliet. Marriage is not expected to provide the source of joy and fulfillment in this world – in India there is deep cultural awareness that only the Divine can ultimately satisfy the soul. Marriage has a social function, and intense romantic love is not a prerequisite. Arranged marriages are still the rule, and though bridal abuse and honor killings remain a stain on India's culture, in general, marriage there is able to fulfill its more limited expectations.

At age twenty-five, I knew nothing of this. I only knew that I had met a fellow artist of a deep spiritual dimension, whose counsel helped ground my search for Spirit, whose innate earthly joy called me back from the brink.

I came to marriage with my ancestral model intact, ready to project my parents' missionary partnership onto a new canvas, but one lesson had been well learned. I knew that marriage was not the key to bliss, was not the answer to unmet yearnings, and that a partnership that left God a distant second would not last. I tried to express this to Alicia, tried to articulate that nothing was more important to me, that my life would be empty if I could not somehow find a way into deep divine communion.

I was in love and so, of course, I heard what I wanted to hear, and ignored the signs that warned of days ahead when the greening garden path we walked would diverge, when the very growth and learnings that delighted us at the start would be the loving impetus toward an eventual parting years later. If we had been blessed with children, so much would have changed, for then the karmic consequences magnify and touch other precious lives, and through them still other lives, and the snares of the great game multiply and tighten. For us, there were no children, and so we had only our own growth to nurture, only our own potentials to honor, and only our own consequences to pay.

I am averse to confessional memoirs that drag into sunlit glare the intimate details of one's past loves. The loyalty I still feel to the two remarkable women who shared their lives with me in partnerships that spanned a quarter-century inhibits me from airing the struggles common to all couples. The search for union with Spirit mattered no less to Alicia than to me. It will sound self-serving when I say that our paths diverged finally in ways that seemed divinely guided, but that is my truth. Divorce was not in my lexicon, and it took a years-long geographic separation for the lesson to sink home that for Alicia as for me, we needed the support of our respective spiritual communities to thrive and be happy. I had found that my indispensable spiritual support lay at the other end of the continent. We found at last that neither could ask the other to leave that support in the name of our marriage. Yet, I think that she did not finally believe that I would truly leave her for God (so to speak) until it was too late.

You may wish to know this: the path of union through devotion is finally a solitary and interior journey. No mortal lover, however highly evolved or blissfully inspiring he or she may be, can make this journey for you. The discipline of spiritual practice that opens the door to Her presence you must forge alone. The intimacy with God you must nurture alone. Hours of solitude will be necessary. As the inner communion and ceaseless loving conversation with the Lover become real to you, sustain you, enrapture you, the peace and joyful vitality that you carry back into your life can uplift and transform your marriage and indeed your whole life, but you cannot ask or expect that your mate will carry you to God.

I learned this the hard way. My first marriage ended when my own weakness became intolerable to me, and I saw that I would need solitude and a spiritual community to develop the discipline needed to break through to the Lover's presence.

Romancing the Divine

A three-month professional trip to Los Angeles became a life-transforming immersion in meditation, and the Lover opened many doors and showered many blessings, while my wife waited for me to return.

"Come home!" she cried. "Come join me!" I entreated. Over two and a half years, we finally saw that to return would cripple my soul, and to leave the life and work she had built in order to join me would cripple hers. And so love demanded that we let go.

CHAPTER 22

▲ ▲ ▲

The Lover's Presence

As for me, I want to be in the Divine embrace now. Not next lifetime, not in a theorized heaven I can only imagine, not according to some formula of eventual salvation, but in the constant loving embrace here, now, in this world of troubles and taxes and daily tasks, of the loving divinity that is the Reality behind "reality."

In my longing to be in love with the Divine, I found that it is just as with a mortal lover whom you desire to love. Find ways to please her! Do small things for the love of her!

If you have been in love in this life, you know that in those first flights of love your lover is never far from your thoughts. You work with the thought of how soon you may be together. You steal moments away from distracting tasks so that you may briefly speak with your love. You delight to think of some small thing you may do to bring a smile to her face, and to draw her more closely to you.

The great lovers tell us God is no different. He hungers for our love more avidly than we can imagine. Every little gesture touches Him more deeply than we can know. Every moment taken to talk with Him is as sweet — and sweeter — to the Infinite Lover's heart than the warmest moment of stolen intimacy your memory can summon.

You will find, with only a little searching, a beautiful literature of love on the subject of the presence of the Lover and how to practice it (you will find

Romancing the Divine

a few that have mattered deeply to me in the Appendix). Yes, it is a practice, and it does not come easily or all at once. It takes years, or even a lifetime, to perfect. But we are reminded often by the great lovers that the Divine is present even from the very beginning, that God responds even to our first humble efforts. We simply need to be alert for that response, those first visitations of peace, of love, to be alert to recognize those moments of divinely arranged help in our daily struggles that speak to you of your Lover's presence.

Brother Lawrence said we ought to act with God in the greatest simplicity, speaking to Him frankly and plainly, and imploring His assistance in our affairs just as they happen. God never failed to grant it, as Brother Lawrence had often experienced.

CHAPTER 23

The Lake Shrine

THE SAINTS I'VE known warned us not to share experiences. I mean those sacred ones that are intimate moments between you and God, moments of bliss, of vision, or of favors. You will very often find that those moments lose something of their sanctity and special intimate quality if you speak of them too freely to others. Jesus spoke of this, of those who pray in public in order to be seen as pious, that they already have their small reward. But He urged us to "pray to your Father in secret, and in secret He will reward you."

As for me, I would one day be asked to often "pray in public" (and to lead others in devotional chant) and would experience the temptation of that small reward of being thought holy by others. I observed how I grew to expect those small ego rewards — someone waiting after the meditation to tell me how inspired they were, or *pronaming* to me in the same reverential way that I would to the Reverend Mother - and then caught myself looking for such rewards with eagerness. Much as I would struggle to pray and chant only from the heart, and to be grateful for the privilege, the human desire for recognition would reassert itself, and then I would feel ashamed.

But I gradually saw that the shame itself was the ultimate ego trap. "O, what a sad case I am!" I would tell myself. "How unworthy of grace!"

And then I came across this quote:

> *"Once I heard it said that there was more of self-love than desire for penance in such sorrow."*

— ST. TERESA OF AVILA

Romancing the Divine

St. Teresa saw through this one too, long ago. How much easier simply to accept that I would fall in this way, being merely human, and to trust that God would lift me up again and again, and would finally lift me beyond this fault through sheer grace, merited or not. I was finally able simply to be glad if others were inspired, thank them, and let it go. I gradually learned that the Lover didn't mind that my love was so imperfect. She sees our efforts, and knows our hearts.

So then, about sharing intimate spiritual experiences with others: how would you feel if your lover boasted to others of moments you considered sacred and intimate? Divine Mother feels the same way – She might delay to visit you again, if you do not treat Her love with reverence.

For myself, it was a dilemma in this book. I feel it right to share some stories, but not others. There is nothing more private, more sacred than the experiences that the Divine grants you in this romance. The more you press them to your heart with gratitude and reverence, the deeper will your intimacy become. Occasionally you may be speaking with a fellow lover of God, and be moved to share a personal story for their encouragement, as I feel moved now.

I had moved from Chicago to Los Angeles – ostensibly to pursue my still thriving acting career – but soon found it was another pull that moved the journey. I had found a modest apartment near the church where Brother Bhaktananda served as minister, and found work with a courier service. I heard Brother speak in his quiet and powerful way about the bliss that comes to those who practice the presence of the Divine, and I was on fire to follow his example.

Like Brother Lawrence, Brother Bhaktananda found that he did not need to neglect the Beloved during times of work, that he could keep his attention on God even while engrossed in demanding duties.

I often thought to myself, however, that neither the saintly monk of 17th century Paris, nor Brother Bhaktananda, had tried to practice the presence of God while driving forty hours a week in L.A. traffic with a stack of boxes and

Michael Henry Dunn

a massive map book perched on the passenger seat! (This in the days before the GPS, before Google, and just before the prevalence of cell phones.)

In those forty hours, I would more often take the name of God in vain than in prayer. Yes, I more often invoked His ire upon the heads of those who dared to cut me off than I did to gently ask His blessings on my "fellow passengers to the grave," as Dickens put it. (For your comfort, and in my defense, I will reveal that even certain very highly evolved souls I have known have confessed to succumbing to the serenity-wrecking challenges of the Santa Monica Freeway on occasion!)

But of course, the Lover loves to test our love, and so I tried very hard. I would return home after a day of stress sufficient to age me a decade, take a candlelit bath to restore the body, then stagger to the meditation garden to try to recover my lost equanimity.

One April day my frustration reached a zenith. In the Hollywood Hills, the reclusive and exclusive hideaways on Mulholland Drive do not advertise their driveways or their addresses in the ordinary, middle-class fashion. A half-hidden plank obscured by a shrub may hold five or six illegible addresses on it. Lovely if you seek privacy - insanity-provoking if you seek to deliver a package…particularly if your profit margin dwindles with every mile lost to fruitless meanderings. All the while, of course, attempting to keep a silent river of devotion flowing peacefully through your mind.

To be brief, I lost it.

A passerby would have witnessed a 1988 blue Dodge Daytona pulled over in the dust, with a lone man in the front seat (nearly obscured by a stack of undelivered boxes) screaming highly colorful language while gesticulating wildly toward the heavens.

The screams comprised a kind of prayer. I was addressing God in very emphatic language. It went something like this: "*%#&! If You don't give me a &#$! job where I can practice your *&%$ presence, I'm going to…I'm going

Romancing the Divine

to...well, I don't know what the &^%$ I'll do, but You'd better help me here, G--d----t!"

It was, you see, a sincere prayer. Deep, passionate, and very sincere.

And so, of course, She answered.

This dream held no light, or bliss. Joy, yes, but of a gentle sort. That night I dreamed I was visiting the monastery where Brother Bhaktananda had once lived. I walked into the main building, and there was the Reverend Mother of the order sitting in a large chair, doing some knitting. She looked up and saw me, and smiled warmly. She gestured me to come a little closer, and then said in a kind of conspiratorial whisper, "I've said a prayer for you!"

I smiled with surprised joy and *pronamed* to her. Then I turned to find Brother Bhaktananda standing to one side. He too leaned in confidentially and whispered, "Consider yourself employed!"

I did not often dream of saints and so I woke with the dream still vivid in my mind. The meaning was a bit obscure, but the joy of it lingered.

It might have been that day, or the day after. On my daily post-courier stagger towards the meditation chapel, I saw a notice posted on the community bulletin board: "Wanted: Male Vegetarian Cook or young man willing to learn." Little paper strips with a phone number clung to the notice, with no other indication of the employer. Young I still was, willing I certainly was, a cook I was not (though I had flipped burgers in a theater bar in NY). I took a strip with the phone number, and decided to give it a try.

The job was in the monastery. Within a week the Reverend Mother herself was signing my paycheck. And the kitchen where I was to work was located in a lakeside meditation garden world-famed for its peace and beauty, a place of such powerful sanctity that few can visit it unchanged, which would become my spiritual home for the next twenty years.

The Self-Realization Fellowship Lake Shrine, Pacific Palisades, California

If I couldn't practice the presence of Divine Mother there (She may have reasoned), I was probably on the wrong planet.

So sometimes it's good to have a screaming fit with God. It's not the generally recommended practice, I know, but as long as you are conversing with the Divine from the heart, you can't really go wrong.

CHAPTER 24

▲▲▲

Meditation and Money

I HAVE KNOWN men of the world who then became monks. I have known monks who returned to the world — sometimes after cloistered decades. Beset by the burdens and distractions of modern life and its attendant pursuit of money and status, the monastery beckons as a haven of holy safety, and seeming security. Once in the monastery, much of this burden is lifted, but the spartan simplicity and solitude of monastic life can leave an aching emotional void for those who are not suited to such an existence (and it is my experience that few are truly so suited). Drawn back out into the world in the hope of human love, I have seen them find it...and with it suddenly the necessity of income, the reality of bills, the needs of a wife, the startling reality of children. And the longing for divine communion often fades amid the clamor to a ghostly whisper in a haunted soul.

One winter night in the forest below the hill town of Assisi, eight centuries ago, Francesco Bernadone struggled in his little monastic hut with the desires of the flesh. He had been the Prince of Revels once, the prankster, the singer, the ardent troubador beneath many a lover's window. He had been far from the handsomest lad in the town, but he possessed an unsurpassed charm of personality. When the Divine seized his soul, and his beloved became Lady Poverty, he took with him into the forest the memory of those romantic nights, and on occasion these memories would rise irresistibly in his mind, and with them the yearnings of the body, and the loneliness of the heart.

On this night, as it happened, there was a witness to his torment, and so the story has come down to us. Another monk lay awake in his own hut, and so he heard the tossing and turning of his spiritual father, Francesco, in the nearby hut (and mere huts they were, too – so small that the monks' legs would often stick out the door as they slept). On a sudden, Francesco sprang up from where he lay, emerged naked in the snowy chill, and threw himself on the ground, rolling in the snow itself, furiously intent on mastering the body's heated demands.

Still struggling with his desires, he arose and frenziedly rolled the snow into a snowman – or snow-woman as it appeared – and setting it up, he exclaimed aloud, "You want a wife, Francesco? There she is!"

He swiftly built another. "A servant, Francesco? There he is!"

And two more, small ones. "And children, Francesco? You want children? There they are! Wife, servant, children – you have them all!"

"Now, Francesco! Go out, and support them!"

And with that he returned to his hut. If he had returned to Assisi to assuage his lonely longings, we would never have heard of him.

Later, his irresistible blend of a troubador's passion with an apostle's zeal would prove so seductive to the people of Italy that a "Third Order" would arise so that those with family responsibilities who yearned to love God as the "Little Poor One" did could embrace his way of life.

Like them, I wanted to have it all. Monastic simplicity and devotion, minus obedience, minus seclusion, minus celibacy (and as it turned out, minus children). But I was not living in a forest hut below 12th century Assisi, but in late 20th century Los Angeles.

I could berate myself (and have often done so) for lacking the purity of purpose that drove St. Francis, or for allowing my desire for a life of monastic simplicity to be compromised by the desire to please a wife, or for allowing the devotional discipline I acquired in those years at the shrine to be weakened by the stressful demands of making a living, or for allowing debt to pile up with the easy credit of the '90s – and the insanely easy credit of the decade after.

After excessive self-blame it is human nature to segue into self-absolving rationalization, and so I have often excused myself that I had no tutoring in how to handle money, that my childhood experience of money entailed no apparent lack of it and endless anxiety concerning it, that I had come to believe that as a "spiritual person" the Divine Hand would always provide my needs (as indeed She often did). But the cold truth is that anxiety over money directly impeded the flow of abundance in my life, and that progress toward Divine intimacy was often choked off by the stress of financial hardship.

My guru taught "plain living and high thinking" – to live simply within one's means, to create a prudent reserve of savings, and to avoid "unnecessary necessities" – the pursuit of which complicates life and shuts out time for God-communion.

The Western world is now reeling with the shock of absorbing these precepts, for the pursuit of "unnecessary necessities" has been the fuel driving the global economy, and the reckless accumulation of debt beyond one's means now threatens to topple the world financial system.

I learned these lessons only via the same shocking ordeal as millions of others. I learned that one cannot "pray away" one's debts – but that spirituality and money can be integrated in a powerfully healing way. It took me many years and cost much pain, and I needed every hidden touch of the Divine Hand to do it, but the lessons are finally taking hold.

I have no expertise or authority in these things, and excellent resources are ready to hand for those who wish to adopt "plain living and high thinking." I only know that without such balance, we will far oftener be crying in fear for the Lover's help from a place of anxious stress than communing with Him in the serene silence of meditation.

I also know that as long as I never ceased asking for that help, it was always provided, until the lesson was learned.

CHAPTER 25

▲▲▲

Years in the Monastery Kitchen

ARE THE GREAT heights of blissful union as open to the householder as to the monk or nun? My life has been a quest to experience an answer to this question.

You may indeed find that only the complete surrender of celibacy will satisfy your soul. This book may perhaps turn out to be just one step on a path that leads you ultimately to let go of the desire for human love, to find your way to a cloistered spiritual community wherein you may focus on God alone. If so, you have my admiration and heartfelt prayers. It is not an easy road.

In my years in the monastery kitchen, I dwelt in both worlds at once, in a way. I lived alone adjacent to monastery grounds, but I wore a wedding ring. I worked in silence with monks, meditated with them every morning, and cooked their midday meal, but I was not cloistered and I was not celibate. In those first two years, my wife would come from Chicago to spend a weekend every couple of months. Though I would socialize with other devotees on the weekend, my married status and my work in the monastery served to protect me from becoming distracted by the temptation of other relationships.

Michael Henry Dunn

The author in the monastery kitchen at the SRF Lake Shrine, 1993

And I saw the monks around me struggle silently with the same questions and the same doubts that haunted me. Of the twelve monks whose meals I cooked when I arrived, six had left the monastery within a few years, all of them to marry.

But this was no ordinary monastery. Though all the essentials of monastic life were in place – celibacy, simplicity, obedience, prayer, meditation, work – the monastic environment was compromised by one very significant fact: a renowned meditation garden open to the public a few hundred yards from the beach at the southern edge of Malibu.

Monasticism, by definition, involves isolation from the opposite sex. For eight hours of the day, the grounds welcomed devotees, tourists, the curious, and the lightly clad (modest attire by Malibu standards could still be fairly

Romancing the Divine

provocative). It was said that the Shrine was the place where the Order sent monks to be tested.

And tested they were. One infamous starlet (well-known at the time for her shamelessly self-promoting Sunset Boulevard billboards) would frequently pull into the meditation gardens in a pink Corvette, and flounce onto the grounds, exposing to the legal limit every last square inch of a notoriously abundant figure. A call would go out over the grounds patrol radio – "Angelyne alert! Angelyne alert!" Some desperately blushing monk or volunteer would on occasion have to politely offer her a shawl, reminding her that she was on church grounds.

And it seemed that God delighted to arrange such tests. One poor fellow I knew, a very earnest and reticent young monk, was asked to temporarily relieve the parking valet in the shrine's parking lot. Looking a bit out of place in his monastic tunic, he stood awkwardly at the gate, waving in the cars. Whereupon, a tall attractive blonde walked in the gate, straight up to him, and without so much as a "hello" planted a kiss smack on his mouth! The poor man nearly fainted with the shock. And then he was desperately afraid that the monk in charge might have seen, fearing that he would at once be sent to monastic Siberia (yes, there was such a place) through no fault of his own.

Though embarrassing, the visual distractions that would stroll in from the beach at the Shrine were actually easier for the monks to ignore than the experience of meeting sincerely spiritual women at meditations or services. For the natural magnetism between the sexes does not decrease in the early stages of meditation, but grows stronger. Divine Mother's beauty becomes more attractive, not less.

My tests were of a different nature. The kitchen was in a shed on a hilltop overlooking the shrine, and I worked in something more like monastic isolation.

I had no idea where my life was going. I had no idea if my marriage would survive. My ambitions for a life as an actor were rapidly fading. When I accepted the job as cook, the monk in charge explained to me, "You see, Michael, it helps morale if the food is good. We're monks, we've given up a lot of pleasures most people take for granted, which is fine…but we really can't have our cook running off at a moment's notice to go be a movie star." He asked for a commitment of a year.

"You are working in a place of an extremely high spiritual vibration," he told me. "Our guru communed deeply with Divine Mother on these grounds, and those vibrations remain. If you spend a year in this environment - you will change."

I saw the power of the place work on others. More times than I can count, strangers to the grounds, who knew nothing of its history, would spend an hour in the powerful peace of the lakeside gardens, and then ask, "What is it about this place?" A mysterious inner cleansing and upliftment would take place, which they were often powerless to describe.

I felt a longing to spend hours meditating on those grounds, to soak up that peace, to instill devotional discipline in my recalcitrant spine. Ironically, by the time my duties in the isolated kitchen were at an end, the grounds were closed to the public – which meant me. At 5 p.m., the grounds reverted to being a monastic cloister, and even lay disciples were expected to leave. I was taken aback. I had won, seemingly by some blend of merit and desperation, the privilege of working in this environment. But Brother Devananda, the monk in charge, said that the most I would be allowed to do was meditate for an hour or so in the bushes at the top of the stairs which led down to the shrine.

I tried it. It was not edifying. I was sitting in a bush. Bugs and a bad view, and the sound of buses and motorcycles on nearby Sunset Boulevard.

I considered again Brother's stand. These men had, after all, embraced a cloistered life with the intention of living a life of simplicity and solitude, which was badly compromised by the public meditation gardens as it was. The environment was not merely about solitude – it was supported by the presence of those also committed to celibacy and service. And after hours their privacy was supposed to return to them, the support of their monastic seclusion in place. And the sight of me with my wedding ring, and my periodic conjugal visits with the absent wife, me with my freedom to go out to a movie if I chose, or to skip a meditation if I chose, yet with the privilege of sharing their monastic grounds, free to meditate with them in the mornings, seemingly enjoying all the benefits of monastic life with little of the sacrifice....well, let's just say it may not have been good for morale.

"Well," I thought, "what if I were completely invisible?"

That is how I found my cave.

I will not tell you where it was. I don't want to be responsible for people clambering over the off-limits sections of those sacred grounds, looking for that hidden place of shaded solitude by the water. I will tell you that a rope was necessary to lower oneself into it – a rope which is no longer there. The massive tree that disguised the place is gone now too. I found that I was completely hidden from view, and yet could meditate mere feet from the lake. The shrine to world peace containing the ashes of Mahatma Gandhi was only yards away. A small box tucked beneath some leaves held my meditation blanket. My only companions were three swans and a few dozen turtles. And as I quieted the breath, my mind would begin to absorb the peace of the place as the sun set and the moon rose, and my *sadhana* began in earnest.

However, I couldn't very well sneak onto the grounds to meditate – I needed Brother's permission. I explained my discovery to him, and emphasized that the worst intrusion I would make would be in that brief half-minute as I descended to my hiding place from the hilltop kitchen.

He consulted with his brother monks. A carefully limited permission was given.

It sounds idyllic, I know. And it was very beautiful. Looking back, those days seem so ideal – my brief interlude of quasi-monastic freedom between marriages, when my heart began to become still enough so that the reality of the Lover could be felt, when I began to think that perhaps the monastery would be my home after all.

I remember arising from two hours of meditation one night, and peering up through the guardian tree at the dazzling fullness of the moon, absorbed in a stillness so powerful that the sounds of Sunset Boulevard were somehow muted to perfect silence.

One night the vibrations of peace suddenly became ten times as powerful, while the world around me went briefly mad.

Light Amid the Violence – The Riots of 1992

In April of 1992, I completed my first year of work in the monastery. I commuted from the meditation center where I lived (in Hollywood) to the one where I worked – a forty-minute drive. One day I noticed an iron-grilled fence, decorative but imposing, going up around the chapel by my home, with a heavy steel door where once there had been an open church entrance.

I was appalled. "What's their problem?" I wondered. "Do they expect rioting hordes to come pillaging down Sunset Boulevard and storm the chapel?"

Two weeks later, the four L.A. policemen on trial for the Rodney King beating were acquitted on all counts. Los Angeles exploded into the worst riots of the 20th Century. Fifty people were killed. Smoke rose from a hundred unchecked fires as snipers took shots at firemen. And rioting hordes did indeed come pillaging down Sunset Boulevard to the door of the chapel.

It was a Thursday night, the night of the weekly devotional service, and one foolhardy volunteer usher thought it might be a good idea to stand in front

Romancing the Divine

of the new chapel gate on Sunset in the middle of the riots, in his suit and tie. A pick-up truck loaded with rioters pulled up at the sight of him. A gun was pointed and fired.

It misfired. They drove on.

At the Lake Shrine that night, a sense of panic could be felt in the streets as drivers became reckless in their anxiety to seek the refuge of home. Lines formed at gas pumps, and at markets as people stockpiled essentials, fearful of the chaos. Rumors spread that rioters had invaded Beverly Hills and were headed west. The long drive home to Hollywood would take me right through areas where convenience stores were being torched and looted, and where the police had largely lost control.

My cave beckoned. The thought of spending the night there was tantalizing. In this emergency, common sense said not to bother the monks with the question of permission. Within the perimeter of the shrine, as I climbed into my cave, the noise of the fear-stricken traffic receded and became a child's faint night-time cry, an echo only of the nightmare that was consuming Los Angeles.

After practicing the techniques for stilling the mind, I gazed (as I had been taught) at the Spiritual Eye in the forehead. There, for the first time in my life, I saw it blaze (exactly as my guru had said it would) in a steady brilliance, the golden light surrounding the blue center, and within, the star. A powerful peace seemed to flow out from the light and envelop my being, as if the great souls who blessed the shrine were pouring out their protective blessings on the troubled city, through this one holy portal. I felt gratitude, deep gratitude and reassurance, as my soul bathed for the first time in the light of the source from which we all have sprung.

And then, as my karma would have it, one of the gardeners called my name from the nearby path, disturbing my concentration, and the light faded.

I struggled to refocus, to let myself fall into this beauty for which I had longed for so many years, but the moment was now gone. Reluctantly, I pulled myself up by the rope to the hidden entrance, and appeared on the path. A bed was available, I was told, at a nearby home, if I preferred not to spend the night in the open. This too was protection, I realized, and I accepted.

But I've often wondered, in the years since, what would have unfolded, how deep would I have gone if I had simply remained rooted where I was, ignoring the body's demands, and had surrendered to the powerful light and peace that the Divine was pouring out upon the shrine during the riots of 1992. The Light has come often again since then, but never (or at least not yet) with such a sense of presence and purpose.

I trust it will not need another heinous calamity for me to connect that deeply again. But it would often happen in the years to come that the Lover would remind me of Her protective presence when my foolhardy behavior had placed me in peril.

CHAPTER 26

▲▲▲

The Lover to the Rescue

As you grow closer to your Lover, and avidly practice the presence of the Beloved, you may find that the Divine hand becomes more apparent in your life, and the Divine protection more vigilant.

Does Divine Mother then play favorites, and protect some of Her children while neglecting others?

I would say that when we turn to the Divine with dedication, humility, and passion, the ever-present loving protection that She extends to all of us simply has less interference in its way, and can manifest more directly, more personally.

How to Make a Death Trap

One day in the monastery kitchen I received an unexpected phone call. It was from Brother Bimalananda, a delightful Italian-American monk in his seventies, a diminutive pixie of a man whose blissful passion for Divine Mother made him a bit of a loose cannon in the eyes of his fellow monks. His eyes were amazing deep wells of purity and joy. He and Brother Bhaktananda were like divine twins, but Bimalananda was effusive and a bit eccentric where Bhaktananda was quiet and reserved.

Brother Bhaktananda (left) and Brother Bimalananda

I had only met him once or twice, and as he was a senior monk, revered by all, had no connection to my kitchen duties, and resided at a different location, I was a bit startled that he asked for me by name. He said he understood that I was going on retreat that weekend to the monastic ranch near San Diego, and wondered when I was returning to Los Angeles. "Sunday night," was the answer.

"Oh, I see. Golly, I was hoping it was Monday morning, as I need a ride up to Los Angeles at that time."

The prospect of chauffeuring this saintly and delightful monk prompted me to offer to stay another night, and come back Monday, as I was not scheduled to work at the monastery that day. He was quick to take me up on it, and we arranged to meet at noon on Monday.

I thought it a bit odd, as there were many monks at the ranch, many monastic vehicles, and presumably many people eager to do a favor for a

Romancing the Divine

saint. Why he should have called me, and how he knew I was coming to the ranch I did not know.

I lived at this time in a garden studio apartment in Santa Monica, a simple and sunny place that suited me to the bones. It was plainly furnished with a couch-bed, and a broad coffee table that I had converted by means of stacked-up planks and cinder-blocks into a make-shift entertainment center several shelves high, supporting a cheap second-hand television, a cassette player, and sundry books and statuary. Behind this precarious structure, a massive bronze mirror left behind by the previous tenant leaned against the wall, giving the room a more spacious look. Another large mirror came with the place, secured to the wall behind the couch-bed. This mirror caused me some anxiety, as I feared it would come crashing down on my head in the event of a night-time earthquake. I had made a little mental note that if this were to happen, I would move quickly towards the foot of the bed with a pillow over my head. Two strong earthquakes had shaken Southern California little more than a year before, and I did not take them lightly.

The monastic ranch was idyllic. Set in the high country above Escondido, a hundred miles south of Los Angeles, it is a place of wonderful sunny quiet, a simple hardworking lifestyle for the monks and residents, and a refreshing retreat for visitors. I spent two deeply restful days in this perfect haven, with the added blessing of being able to stay for the long meditation Sunday night, since I was staying over the extra night at Brother Bimalananda's request.

Very early the next morning, Monday, January 17th, 1994, at around 4:30 a.m., I was roused by the gentle sound of my teacup on the nightstand rattling mildly for a moment. An earthquake, I realized…a small one. Or, I mused, rather than a small nearby quake, it might be a large one far away. I got up, quickly dressed, and went outside. The valley was quiet, and the sky was madly splashed with stars. I felt moved to visit the tiny chapel in the garden to meditate.

Had I been at home, I would likely have been killed. The mild rattle of my teacup in Escondido was the 7.4 deadly Northridge temblor in Los Angeles. Those who lived through the quake described it as unlike any other they had experienced...as if a giant had seized their building and were shaking it up and down like a toybox. Grand pianos were said to leap around living rooms like jumping beans.

I had absent-mindedly constructed a death-trap in my little garden dwelling, directly in front of my bed, made of loose cinder blocks, planks, and a massive bronze mirror leaning loosely behind it. In my anxiety to flee the mirror secured behind me (which, in the event, remained secured), I would have moved directly into the path of this deadly cascade of concrete and glass.

Instead, I got a call from a saint, and had the quiet blessing of driving him to Los Angeles that morning. I mentioned my relief to Brother as we drove, hearing reports of the deaths and damage. "Oh, yes. It must have been Divine Mother protecting you," he said – and went back to meditating in the passenger seat beside me.

The Love of Brother Bimalananda

I must tell you more of Brother Bimalananda. "Life is chiefly service," his Master often said, and Brother Bimalananda did not allow a dearth of duties in his old age to keep him from finding a way to serve the Divine. Even into his frailer years you could find him sweeping the street in front of the monastic headquarters – not the sidewalk, the street itself – while singing "O Sole Mio" in a lusty tenor. The Beloved was such a moment-to-moment Reality to him that his conversation was unaffectedly sprinkled with reference to Her. Once a friend of mine was with him as they passed a flatbed truck carrying a massive, odd-looking, unidentifiable piece of machinery tied down with cable.

"I wonder what Divine Mother wants with that?" he mused.

Another time, a brush fire swept through the high country near the monastic ranch. Thousands of acres were consumed, along with hundreds of dwellings. Firefighters told the monks to evacuate – there was nothing they could do to stop the approaching blaze. The ranch, the cabins, the monastery, the chapel, the fields that fed the monks and nuns – all would be lost.

At this news, Brother Bimalananda calmly went out onto the lawn in front of the refectory, and faced the direction of the approaching conflagration. This frail little old man then raised his arms toward the fire, and began to quietly chant the Name of God.

Hour after hour, without lowering his arms, Brother Bimalananda invoked Divine protection. Other monks, inspired by his example joined him as the afternoon wore on and the danger grew. The fire came roaring over the hill, racing down the slope toward the ranch. Still Bimalananda kept up his chant. At the property line itself, the fire simply stopped…and went out.

Aerial photographs of the fire will show you the high country totally consumed – except for one unburned area that traces the property line of the ranch, completely encircled by charred ruin.

The monk in charge of the property put it succinctly: "Brother saved the ranch."

To Brother Bimalananda, Divine Mother saved the ranch.

How Not to Sleep

Another time I had the fortune to be on retreat at the ranch while Brother Bimalananda was there. His room was a couple of doors down from mine on an outdoor porch. He could be seen gaily traversing the property on an old bicycle, on his mysterious rounds.

Michael Henry Dunn

Paramahansa Yogananda taught his disciples about the proper way to sleep. Do not sleep on your left side, he cautioned – the magnetism in that direction is not helpful, and can generate disturbing dreams. Facing the right is better. But sleeping on your back with your hands at your side is best for complete rest of mind and body.

I had tried in vain to practice this, and I often ended up curled up facing left. At the ranch it was even more difficult. The bed was standard issue monastic fare: a hard flat board beneath a none-too comfy mattress, but it was fine with me, if a bit small.

One night in the little cabin room off the porch, in the deep middle of the night, I had a terrible dream. Like the Dutch boy in the legend, I had my fist in a dam, trying to hold back a terrible flood. In my terror, I knew that the dam wall was about to break, and that I would drown along with all my people. In my dream I called out in panic to the Divine for help. As I mentally screamed for aid, I became aware that I was lying on my left side, my body jammed against the wall, caught in the space between the wall and the bed.

In that half-conscious paralyzed state between fearful dream and wakefulness, I heard footsteps out on the porch.

"Oh, no!" I thought in confusion, "It's Brother Bimalananda! I don't want to bother him!" But still I was caught in the terror of the dream, jammed between the bed and the wall, trying to hold back the ocean itself – trapped in that fearful state of paralysis wherein one's life force is so withdrawn into the brain in sleep that the body refuses to obey even the most urgent command of the suddenly awakened mind. I was aware of not wanting to bother Brother, but still I had to save my dream people from the dream flood that stormed against my illusory dam – caught in the negative energies, it seemed, of sleeping the wrong way! And still I screamed an agonized prayer to the Divine to save me.

Even so, I heard Bimalananda's footsteps approach. The sound stopped outside my door.

At that moment, I suddenly felt a warm vibrating glow in my chest, centered in my heart. This glow grew into a powerful vibration of joy, which literally and physically lifted me half a foot up in the air, removed me from the vise of wall and bed, and gently turned me over onto my back in the middle of the bed. The nightmare at once receded, and my fear vanished.

"Oh, thank you!" I whispered, and drifted back to sleep.

Outside, the footsteps retreated and I heard Bimalananda's door close.

It was only a little miracle of modest levitation, a small kindness to ease my sleep, done effortlessly, anonymously, and lovingly by one whose oneness with the Divine has given him the power to be, when She wills, Her channel.

A Mother's Day Disguise

One Mother's Day, not long ago, I joined some friends for a long afternoon of chanting and meditating. Being the day it was, we chanted Her Name over and over, and the peace in the chapel was deep and full - full of the Divine Mother's mercy and love.

Afterward, I took my laptop to a cafe to work on a project. I had recently acquired a scooter – a sturdy Indian-made Bajaj *Chetak* – and fancied myself both clever and cool as I tooled about the unsafe streets of Los Angeles' West Side. Done with my work that night, I climbed aboard the scooter to return to the beach house where I lived on Pacific Coast Highway, where I discovered to my chagrin that I had somehow dropped my house keys along the way. I returned to the cafe and searched in vain. I returned to the house and searched in vain again, depositing my laptop on the porch. Unwilling to give up, I decided to head up the canyon one last time to see if I might have dropped the keys in the parking lot.

Now, I was not the best motorcyclist that walked the earth. I had already, in fact, taken a fall or two, and friends were urging me to reconsider the wisdom of the scooter, pointing out that it was a perfect choice if you lived in a small town in Italy, and tantamount to suicide if you were traveling Sunset Boulevard. But the wind in my hair, and the brilliant economy of the thing had won out.

There is a long green mile of canyon road between the beach and Sunset Boulevard in Pacific Palisades – most of it parkland, full of picnickers during the day, and quite deserted at night. It was now 10:30 p.m., and there was not a soul in sight, nor a car to be seen. Nothing could be safer.

I turned up the canyon road and accelerated briskly, enjoying the cool night air. About three hundred yards up the canyon, my enjoyment was distracted by an odd clicking sound. A fear leaped into my head: I had unloosed the bungee cord that secured my laptop, and the sound would be the knocking of the loose hook of the cord against the spokes of the wheel as I sped up the canyon. If the hook caught in the spokes, the bike would flip over in an instant.

I carefully looked down and behind me to verify my fear: yes, it was true! The cord was loose and knocking against the wheel. I looked up again – to find myself in the gutter, the scooter hugging the curb, where a stream of water now splashed against my legs. My slight lean down to look at the wheel had shifted my weight on the bike to the right, and I had swerved in that brief blind moment from the center of the road to the curb, and lost control.

I attempted to correct the swerve, to regain control, but it required the nerve to accelerate, and I was too inexperienced to know this. I suddenly knew that I would crash, and that nothing could stop it. As the bike spun out of control, and in the brief moment before I hit the pavement, the power of the day's vibration —the many hours of chanting to Motherhood of God - surged up in me and I shouted out, "Mother! Mother! Mother!"

I fell. I rolled over several times, and landed on my feet, unhurt, stunned, and disbelieving.

And then I heard a woman's voice.

"Are you all right?"

Dazed, I looked up at the canyon walls, wondering if this voice could possibly come from one of the houses up there, though they were at least seventy yards away. It seemed the only source, for the canyon was deserted.

And then she stepped out from behind a tree about five yards away.

It was dark, and I couldn't see her clearly. She seemed middle-aged, and was wearing dark clothes, and stood there calmly, waiting for me to answer. There was no one else in sight, no car she might have arrived in, and no indication of how she came to be there, or what she might have been doing alone in the canyon at this hour.

My first response was embarrassment. Here I was, on a deserted canyon road, having crashed a scooter in a brilliant display of ineptitude while screaming for Mother! But still the cry had been from the heart, and I did not want to disavow Her.

So I said, "Well, yes, thank you, I guess I'm OK...you must have heard me just now. There is, after all, one person we call on when in trouble, isn't there?"

There was a moment of silence. She just stood there looking at me. Then she said, "I must say, it was rather funny to see you fall like that, all by yourself."

"Yes, I would think so!" said I. I fumbled with an explanation about the bungee cord, went over to set the scooter upright, climbed aboard, and turned to her again.

"Well then," she said, "If you're all right, I'll just get back to what I was doing."

I thanked her, and turned to start down the canyon, but paused, as curiosity finally caught up with me, and I turned back again to see just what it was she had been doing, alone in the canyon so late at night.

She was walking back toward the woods, picking up leaves from the ground with her bare hands.

And then as I rolled the broken scooter silently down the canyon, the eeriness of it all came to me. The deserted canyon, the lateness of the hour, my frightened call to Divine Mother for help, my miraculously safe fall, and the sudden appearance of this strange woman from behind a tree, almost as if in answer to my call, only a few feet from where I fell.

On Mother's Day, a day spent chanting and meditating on the Motherhood of God.

Caught up in these musings, I walked the scooter along the shoulder of Pacific Coast Highway...until my foot struck metal with a tinkling sound. My keys!

I've driven that canyon road a hundred times at night since, but I've never seen her again.

She can be explained away, of course. She may have been just a homeless woman in the right place at the right time (though She has let me know by touch many times that it was not so). Does that make her any less

Romancing the Divine

miraculous? If you would call upon the Divine Mother of the Universe itself for help, you must not deny Her the right to come to you in whatever form she chooses.

CHAPTER 27

The Restoration of Chivalry

ONE DAY WHEN I was about fifteen years old, I was in the car with my mother. The question of the size of our family had somehow arisen - perhaps we were discussing the chaos that reigned in her life (and by extension in ours) due to the demands of raising ten children (all of us born in a thirteen year span), while also dedicating herself full-time to the bio-chemical evaluations of the children in my father's holistic pediatric practice near Chicago - while also overseeing our 263-acre dairy farm in western Wisconsin.

She explained in a matter-of-fact kind of way that, while it had been her original teenage dream to be a missionary nun in India, she had opted for the back-up dream of marrying a doctor and having thirteen children, and that she had stopped at the neat number of ten because she felt that this was a sufficient number of offspring to diffuse the great power of her personality which would otherwise have concentrated itself in awesome fashion on a mere handful of vulnerable kids. The demands of her career were similarly justified by the motive of mercy towards her brood. "If there were only two or three of you, dear, and if I had no career, I'm sure I would have warped you!"

I passed over in prudent silence the chance to comment on whether she had warped us after all.

So perhaps I had a natural advantage in revering the Divine Feminine, due to my childhood devotion to the Virgin Mary, blended with a matriarchal household ruled by this remarkable woman. But lest you think that my Irish-Catholic

Romancing the Divine

childhood took place in an environment that was a paragon of advanced feminism, it should be noted that, as Malachy McCourt once quipped, "Ireland is a matriarchy. That's where we look down on our women with reverence!"

Since I am addressing my fellow men now, let us revert for a moment to our heads.

Science has found that the genetic differences between men and women are much greater than first thought - almost as great, in fact, as the difference between the genetic makeup of our species as a whole and that of our nearest primate cousin, the chimpanzee.

Our brains, our metabolisms, our endurance, our resistance to pain, the way we process information, our sense of smell, our response to visual stimuli in mating - all carry a marked difference between man and woman. Women live longer, can endure more pain, are better able to multi-task, and will arrive at decisions by way of feeling-centered expressive sharing and what might be called a matri-focal shared power, in contrast to the male model of linear, authoritative problem-solving.

And so, if you as a man feel the need for a theoretical underpinning to the value and appropriateness of a reverence for woman, you might start with the fact that she is your biological superior!

The great saint of India, the revered Amma, is renowned for giving a motherly divine embrace to all who come to her. Thousands line up for days to receive her blessings. And if you are a man, and your wife is with you, she will beckon you forward first, ahead of your spouse because, as she has said, "the man needs the blessing more."

And what is the blessing she imparts? She will draw you close, hold you for a moment and simply murmur Divine Mother's Name in your ear.

She is said to be a pure channel for the Divine, and so the sound of the Name spoken by such a one carries with it a powerful vibration of love and healing. For many who visit Amma with receptive hearts, an experience of sustained upliftment and joy follows.

And a man's voice could, if he desires it, carry that same vibration of love and reverence whenever he speaks the name of his wife, for she is nothing less than a reflection in his life of the Divine Mother Herself.

Yes, whoever she is, whatever your struggles in your marriage, whatever her failings (or yours to her), she can be to you a channel in your life of God's tenderness, compassion and unconditional love. But only if you consciously choose to see her that way, to revere her in that way, and yes, to serve her in that way.

The Rebirth of Chivalry

If you are a man, and you would be in love with the Goddess – that aspect of the Divine that expresses the feminine and motherly qualities of your Source – then you may find yourself embracing a rebirth of the ideals of chivalry.

For you, then, it is not only the beautiful and spiritual woman that will inspire your reverence, but all women – young and old, plain and fair, of all races, all classes, all creeds.

A story is told of a holy man in India who aroused enmity in certain worldly persons. They plotted to disgrace him, and hired a group of beautiful courtesans to dance for him and seduce him. When these gorgeous creatures came into his presence, he at once knelt at their feet, exclaiming, "Divine Mother has come to visit me in the bodies of these Her daughters!"

Humbled and awed by his purity, the women renounced their former ways, and became his disciples.

Romancing the Divine

If you practice this reverence, you will find, over time, that it becomes a sweet habit and a joy to inwardly bow to the Loving Source of all life each time you behold Her reflected in woman. Here we come to the science of love again, for this is a matter of energy and magnetism. The natural magnetism between the sexes is very strong – stronger even than we are aware, and it operates without our knowledge or our consent.

A story was told at the monastery of how the Master forbade his male and female monastic disciples to speak to one another – their ashrams, their walkways, and their duties were strictly separated, as he cautioned them about the power of this magnetism, and its risks for the celibate. One time a young monk was instructed to serve as chauffeur for an elderly nun on a trip of several hours to the Master's desert retreat. The monk knew that he should maintain silence, but thought to himself how many wonderful spiritual stories the nun could tell him of her years of discipleship with the Master – and besides, as she was elderly, what could be the harm? Sure enough, he managed to draw her out, and they spent a pleasant hour of spiritual conversation.

When the monk drove up to the Master's retreat, his omniscient teacher was waiting in the driveway with a stern expression, and at once began to scold him severely for ignoring the prohibition, for treating lightly the magnetism between man and woman. The young monk was at once remorseful and begged forgiveness, at which the Master's scolding melted at once into smiling compassion, a perfect blend of father and mother.

Those of us in the world, who have not chosen celibacy, can still turn our natural inclinations within, can still choose to channel this powerful magnetism rather than repress our natural instincts, and can connect it to the Divine in a wonderfully intimate way.

It is easy enough when I behold a transcendently beautiful woman to see in her a reflection of the Divine. And when those provocative aspects of her beauty

Michael Henry Dunn

speak to my manhood, I do my best to rein in instinct, and reflect for a moment on the question: what is it to which I am drawn here?

If it is the perfection of her body's curves, I remind myself that this instinct was planted in me by evolution, to seek a mate who is apt for child-bearing – one is only being drawn, after all, to her motherhood. If it is the beauty of her eyes, I remember that this image of compassion and nurturing mercy was planted in me as an infant – I am only being drawn, after all, to her motherhood.

I try to make a habit of consciously directing the energy that awakens in that moment, to visualize and feel it moving up the spine in a reverential, prayerful surge, channeling that powerful response toward the higher centers in the heart and brain where the Divine is perceived. If you make a practice of this, you may find that your appreciation of the beauty of woman is enhanced, even as it is purified. And you may find that this response is present for you towards all women, old or young, beautiful or plain. You may find yourself beginning to behave as a knight of old – reverential, chivalrous, respectful.

You may find that you automatically step aside for women in line at the bus, that you naturally and without thinking hold the car door for your wife, that you rise from your table when a lady enters the room. And you may find that the visual seductions that come to you over the internet, or on television – the coarse commercialization and objectification of woman – have less hold on you.

I served as grounds host once at the lakeside meditation gardens I told you of. Passing through the gift shop one day, I saw a tall, dark-haired, statuesque young woman with a very lovely face, and was immediately drawn to her beauty. I smiled at her and walked past, trying to focus on my duties, but her image stayed with me.

A few minutes later, I went to a little grotto nearby to meditate – a secluded place adorned by a statue of the Virgin Mary holding the Christ child. As I walked into the grotto, I saw this same young woman seated by the statue - saw

Romancing the Divine

her in the brief flash of a moment when she bared her breast to nurse her own infant in the privacy of the Virgin's grotto - a perfect image of Divine Mother's nurturing purity.

The sight was breathtakingly beautiful. I at once closed my eyes and bowed in the *pronam* of India, stepping silently away.

Every once in a while, Divine Mother will remind you of who She really is, and how you should really see Her.

It is not a question of equality, of feminism up-ended and turned back by putting woman back on an imprisoning pedestal. The Irish may have once "looked down on their women with reverence," but we can choose to look up to the Divine within both man and woman by seeing Her reflection everywhere.

CHAPTER 28

▲▲▲

For Women: The Bride of God

IN CONVENTS OF old, a nun saw herself as *Sponsa Christi* — the bride of Christ, and her announcement of intention to become a sister was called a "betrothal" — her engagement to God. Is this romantic relationship with the Divine retrievable for women today?

The romance with the Divine is wonderfully rich: He can be to you your Beloved, your Bridegroom, your Father, your Mother, your Friend, even (as we find in India where God takes so many forms) your Child, if that is where your tenderness moves most easily.

It is in India where the image of the Divine as the playful Lover has been vibrantly alive for many centuries for the many women who fall in love with the Lord in the person of Lord Krishna, the irresistibly charming Prince of their hearts, whose flute calls them from their homes to wander in the forests in search of this sweetest of *avatars*, this Divine Seducer of the soul.

The ravishing songs of Mirabai, the poetess-saint of fifteenth-century India, all take as their theme this passionate attachment to Krishna as her lord, her husband, her lover, her all.

Come to my pavilion, O my King.
I have spread a bed made of
delicately selected buds and blossoms,
And have arrayed myself in bridal garb

Romancing the Divine

From head to toe.
I have been Thy slave during many births,
Thou art the be-all of my existence.
Mira's Lord is Hari, the Indestructible.
Come, grant me Thy sight at once.

- MIRABAI

He is all these aspects at once, and all of them put together. Would you deny the One who set the galaxies in motion the power to come to you in any form your heart desired?

The Daughter of God

For each of us in this life, the inclinations of our heart will be formed by our families, by our relationships to our parents, by our environment – and if you believe in reincarnation (it doesn't matter whether you do or not), by your soul history. And the turn our hearts take toward the Divine, the image and relationship that feels natural and right, will arise from the blend of all these influences.

A dear friend of mine simply cannot relate to God as Mother, because her relationship to her own mother in this life was not a warm one. She'll listen to me chant a song to Divine Mother in the chapel sometimes, and say, "You know, that was so beautiful – but somehow I just can't go there. Do you think She'll be mad at me?"

We laugh, and I tell her not to waste her time trying to approach God on a path by which God is not approaching her!

For many in the West, it is easiest to relate to God as a loving Father, for this was the language and relationship of Jesus to God, and Christ remains the great Image for us in the West of union with God.

Michael Henry Dunn

The great Christian prayer of the Our Father (which has its roots in a great Jewish prayer), should tell us at once that we are all sons and daughters of God. Some Christians hold that there was and can only be *one* Son of God, and that it is blasphemy to equate ourselves with Christ.

I am not here to quibble over doctrine. I can only read my New Testament, and see where we are told, "to as many as believed on Him, to them gave He power to become the sons of God." I can only see in the Gospel of John where this greatest Lover of God tells us:

> *And the glory which thou gavest me I have given them; that they may be one, even as we are one. I in them, and thou in me, that they may be made perfect in one; and that the world may know that thou hast sent me, and hast loved them, as thou hast loved me.*
>
> JOHN 17, 22-23, (KING JAMES VERSION)

I can only see the union of Love, of lovers with the Great Beloved – sons and daughters of God.

If Christ and Buddha sat down together, would they quibble over which one was the Son of God?

The Reverend Mother so often would remind us: the path is simple. Love and serve your Beloved.

CHAPTER 29

▲ ▲ ▲

The Lover in Disguise

A FRIEND OF mine walked down Hollywood Boulevard one day in a foul mood. She was addicted to wine but yearned for God, tried to meditate, and had as yet found no way out. She noticed a homeless man, far drunker than she, staggering towards her, gesticulating and shouting gibberish. The sight only made her mood still blacker, and she veered to avoid him. The man suddenly straightened and walked normally – into her path. He stopped in front of her and looked clearly into her eyes.

"You're really only angry at yourself, you know," he said gently.

He then fell back suddenly into his drunken stagger, and wandered off.

The Beloved will not always speak so clearly to you, nor so dramatically use an empty mind as a brief channel to try to reach you, but once you turn firmly toward the Divine, you will begin to hear Her words of guidance coming from the lips of others, if you are in tune.

This same woman, on her frequent trips through the wine aisle of her local supermarket, kept hearing a thought run through her head, like a gentle friendly voice, "the sulfites in wine are bad for you, you know." It became an almost irritating refrain, and this went on for several weeks. One day she visited the lakeside meditation gardens, and encountered Brother Turiyananda, a wonderfully passionate monk who in his early life had run a biker bar in Switzerland. They walked along the lake path and he stopped suddenly, and said, "God wants me to tell you something. The sulfites in wine are bad for you."

She wept.

Michael Henry Dunn

My Words, Her Message

I was at work on a story for a screenplay. It concerned a monk who was tempted by an affair. In the story, the monk gave in to temptation. One Sunday I was on hosting duty in the chapel lobby after the morning service. The lobby was empty as the visiting minister who had given the morning sermon came out from his changing room on his way back to the monastery. As we were acquainted, he asked what I was working on, and I told him of my screenplay. I mentioned that another monk had suggested that I change the story so that the monk did not give in to the temptation of the affair. "For we have too many such stories of moral failure," I said, "What we need is to be inspired by the story of a spiritual man who is tempted, but resists and stays true to his vows."

His face darkened suddenly, and the conversation ended abruptly as he walked quickly from the chapel.

Much later I learned that my story was an exact mirror of his life at that moment, and that he had only the day before given in to the temptation of an affair. I had merely been the unwitting channel of the words God wanted him to hear. (He had been an inspiration to me and many others as a minister, and eventually found his way to an honorable life of service outside the monastery).

It is not only with words of chastisement that the Lover will speak to you through others. Listen for Her also in the words of encouragement, forgiveness, compassion, and praise that come to you from true friends. When you take up the Lover's path, you will find, if you listen, that the Beloved responds to you with marvelous and touching detail.

The Lover in Traffic

I was once wrestling with an agonizing dilemma in my personal life. It had reached a point where it seemed there was no right way forward, and I was near despair as I drove to the meditation gardens one morning along the Coast Highway. "Oh, God," I muttered, "what should I do?"

Romancing the Divine

At that moment a plumber's van passed my car on the left. The banner on its side unfurled past my eyes: "Let the Master take charge…"

God does, you see, have a sense of humor, sometimes to the point of making His response so specific that you cannot possibly mistake Him. Once I was contemplating a trip to The Netherlands, to attend a conference at Utrecht, an old university town. I was driving in West Los Angeles, wrestling with the question of whether I could afford to go, and of whether I could sell enough DVDs of my presentation to cover expenses. I had to make a decision that day to purchase airfare. At that very moment I came up over a rise in the road to face an art supply store's window sign directly in front of me. It read: "Utrecht will not be undersold!"

CHAPTER 30

Chanting and the Battle for Love

OUR HEARTS WILL send us messages by song sometimes. A tune arises in your mind out of nowhere, seemingly, a phrase from a song haunts you, hovers in your brain only half-listened to, and then emerges clearly, insistently, making its way to your lips almost unbidden. And suddenly you may realize that this phrase, this snatch of song is a perfect reflection of an emotional reality in your life – a reality from which you have been hiding. And then there is no silencing the song – it will run on and on, this unrequested message from within, until you silence it by willful distraction.

While I have learned to be open to these inner musical telegrams, I prefer, on the whole, to choose the messages with which my inner singer shall serenade me. For this is a quiet and compelling power - this subterranean river of song can, in fact, carry my mind and my heart where it wishes, if I allow it to meander ungoverned.

Chances are that your mind is under assault by someone else's chant even as you read these words. It may be the last commercial jingle you heard, which is still running amok in your mind. It may be a refrain of complaint from a colleague or supervisor. It may be a song on the radio – one of which you are not particularly fond, but which managed to find the gold standard of "catchiness" that empowered it to run an endless loop in your mind for the better part of a day. There may be a message in these chants that run through you, or they may be mindless. But they are there nonetheless, a subtle influence on your mood, your clarity, and the achievement of your goals.

Romancing the Divine

This is why, when visiting Disneyland, I religiously avoid "It's a Small World After All."

I prefer love songs. Very high love songs - songs to the Lover behind all song. And over the course of my life, the Lover has dropped into my heart sacred songs that have never stopped playing. The music of this inner river carves a deep channel within, and this channel runs on course back to the native ocean for which my soul hungers.

If you are a soul who is swimming upstream anyway – upstream back towards the Lover, upstream against the force of the River of Life running away from Source and out into identification with Form – then you may want to carve a deep channel within that will carry you towards the love you seek.

I would suggest you take control of your inner music, and choose chants that bring you joy, that lift your heart, that carry you toward your highest goals. The right chant, focused in the heart, and integrated into a dedicated spiritual practice, can set you afloat on an inner river of bliss throughout the day – or open the door that leads to God.

This is not an exaggeration.

That is what devotional chant can offer. Some are ancient, some are new. Some have been infused with the spiritualizing power that takes hold of a song forever after if even one holy singer has reached the Beloved by means of that song. Many of them are, for me, bound up with stories – stories of great souls I have known, or stories of lessons I have learned.

There is nothing more powerful than a song. Nothing. The Lover sang you into Being, and maintains your life every moment by the power of the eternally sung Word of Words.

It is up to us to choose what reality we will sing into being in our lives.

Choose your songs carefully. Your inner song is one of the greatest weapons in your hand as one who would overcome the enemies of the Lover.

For to love as we mean to love is to go to battle - to battle against cynicism, against fatigue, against the stress of modernity, against our bad habits, and against the tide of the Ten Thousand Things that would drown our intimacy with the Lover. And this battle is won only by mindful concentration on love, from moment to moment.

What we mean to do is to set the heart silently singing – and to let that song carry you into the arms of the Divine. But a song sung only with the lips, a tune carried mindlessly in the head, will not carry you God-ward. It must spring from your heart in truth and in love.

Taking the Name in Vain

"In vain," of course, simply means without feeling, without reverence. On one level, I'm still just a Chicago Irish kid who loses it on the freeway once in a while, and soils his lips with unholy phraseology – begging Her forgiveness half a moment later! The Lover's vibration, it is true, hums under all words and all sound itself, but She takes no less delight in hearing Her name spoken with tender love than you do.

There is a subtle vibration that lives in a particular chant – and this vibration can then be heightened by the ardor or spiritual realization of the chanter. The legend goes in India that Sri Chaitanya Mahaprabhu, the great saint of medieval times, could bring the entire populace of a town into a state of bliss by the power of his chanting. He had been a phenomenal scholar as a young upper-caste Brahmin boy, besting all the pundits with his perfect knowledge of the scriptures. But then as a young man, he had a sudden devotional awakening, and became an ecstatic devotee of God in the form of Lord Krishna, the beloved savior of India whose enchanting flute calls all souls home to the Divine. He gave up his scholarly fame, took up a bamboo staff, and wandered from village to village, chanting the Holy Name. Tipsy with inner joy, he would arrive on the outskirts of a town, and humbly invite the first person he met to chant with him. He often met with derision, but sooner or later someone would take up the chant, and then his bliss would spread from soul to soul, and by the time he reached the other end of the town, a crowd of blissful hundreds would follow at the heels of this celestial Pied Piper.

In India, it is understood that the vibration of the Divine presence resides within every Name of God. When reverently intoned, a spiritual blessing is imparted. But what does this seemingly trite phrase mean – a spiritual blessing?

It is joy itself, shooting up your spine to your heart, and thence to the crown of your head, lifting your whole being. You can feel it yourself, if you make the experiment. When you utter the name of God, remember as you utter the sound that your body's voice springs from the vibrations of thought, and that the thoughts in your brain are lit by the energy of the sun – for the sun itself by photosynthesis gave rise to every form of life on our planet – and that the sun sprang forth from the Word that God utters forever, echoing from the Primal Shout that gave birth to the cosmos.

There is no separation, no gulf to be bridged, between your voice uttering the Name and the Supreme Reality that the holy sound evokes. If we remember this, and utter the name with focused reverence and devotion, concentrating at the heart, we will feel joy in the chant – for Joy is the essence of the Name, and the essence of our souls.

A Secret of the Name

If you want to always speak the Name with love, I have found a way. When you sit down to meditate, when you breathe deeply, when you calm your mind, and compose yourself to open your meditation with a prayer invoking the Lover's presence, then as you say the words, "Heavenly Father," let the sound of the words as they leave your lips open a vista in your soul wherein you envision that vast uncreated blissful Void beyond Creation in which the Father, the Divine Ground of All Being, the Unmanifest Absolute exists in eternal ecstasy. That this supreme Reality is, in fact, beyond our imagining, does not matter! We are reaching for Him, and the sound of His Name will bring us closer to the One. If you make a habit of this, you will find that, in time, the sound of the Name itself as you speak the word lifts your mind and heart into peace, into joy.

And if you then want to invoke God in the aspect of Divine Mother, if you want to ask Her blessing on your meditation, as you speak Her Name let your mind reach out to all the awesome power of Nature that surrounds you — and then back to the body She gave you. You are giving a soft intimate call to a Lover who is the burning heart of the sun itself — and is the power beating in your heart as well. She has set the earth spinning among the stars, and She is hiding in the sound of your voice as you whisper Her Name. In truth, She is one with your very soul — but you have ceased to remember it.

If you make a habit of this, you may find that in time a rush of bliss at Her beauty will steal your breath before Her Name has left your lips.

Speak the Name of Christ, if He is your love, and see Him enthroned in your heart as you speak, and you will find it so as well. And the name of any great soul who has become one with the One will carry the same vibration, if you speak the words with love and reverence.

By the time your prayer is done, in time you will be half-drunk with God already. And now the power of chant, of a sacred love song, can bring you to the door of communion with Him.

Your song

Choose your songs with care. Choose, or find, or compose, one that touches your heart, that satisfies your need for understanding, that expresses your yearning. And make it simple, with words that can revolve in the back of your mind and heart throughout the day, that you can mindfully return to again and again, that can center you in the heart, that can sing you back to the Presence of the Beloved.

Such a love song becomes a chant. The power of a deeply felt, simple but powerful phrase, sung over and over with feeling from the heart, is known in all cultures, all religions, throughout history. There are battle chants and love chants, rain chants, even money chants, protest chants, football chants, rite-of-spring chants, moonlit madness chants, and chants to guide the soul through the passage of death.

We want a chant that will bring us into the Presence of God.

But the chant alone will take you only so far. It is, as Yogananda said, only half the battle. In the divine romance, chanting is a gift in two great ways: firstly, as a constant inner love song to your Beloved that will keep you in the blissful Presence no matter what daily challenges you face; and then, as the door to meditation, the siren song that lures the wandering thoughts back from the million distractions of the world, that literally shifts the hemispheric dominance in the brain from left to right, from the linear to the intuitive, from logic to love, and prepares your heart for stillness, for deep communion with Spirit as peace, as love, and finally as bliss.

To understand this, we need only remember what it is like to be in love. A song arises in the mind from the sheer exhilaration you feel in thinking of the one you love – some phrase from a love song floats up seemingly out of nowhere, and revolves in your head all the day long. Your step is lighter, you hum through your work with a smile playing on your lips – and your co-workers hide their smiles and roll their eyes at each other knowingly... your secret is not so secret!

The song has carried you into the memory of love, into the presence of the one you adore - and life is beautiful.

Take the Song Within – Then Carry It into Battle

Yes, battle. I am a Gandhi-loving pacifist, but Gandhi well understood that life is a battle, and that there is no struggle more fierce than the one that takes place within us as we strive for the triumph of Love.

I was a trained singer when young. When I left performing behind, and served in the monastery as a cook, I would sing as I worked. Now this is generally not a good idea in a monastery! Not that the monks don't love music – most of them did – but music was for the chapel or for private enjoyment, and if you chose to work in the monastery, you were choosing to work in reverent silence, with your mind on God. But the kitchen was isolated from where the monks worked, and so I would listen to sacred music on a beat-up old cassette player and occasionally sing along as I chopped onions.

Being a singer, chanting struck me as a bit dull – the same thing over and over, with few soaring melodies (or chances to show off!). But Brother Bhaktananda would tell us to chant "with love from the heart," and I began to find that if I truly did this – if I visualized the words of love for God coming from my very heart itself, that before too long, the Lover would steal the breath from the chant in a rush of joy, and I would find myself chanting silently.

That is one secret of chanting – the sooner the chant goes silent, the sooner you fall in love. If you are chanting from the heart - with deep feeling and concentration! – and with your gaze focused firmly but gently at the Spiritual Eye, then let your chant gradually become softer and softer until it becomes a whisper, and then let the whisper become a chant of the mind only...and then you are there!

For it is then just a short step into the peace of meditation. For you have turned the mind within, and have awakened the heart's love, and your eyes can then rise almost effortlessly to gaze gently upward at the Light of God.

You will find it so much easier to meditate if you do this. Your restless mind, your unwillingness, your thousand excuses, your worries and dangers, can all fade away into the background, drowned out by the sweet sound of the Name.

And when your meditation is done, after a time of affirming your love for the Divine, let the peace of your meditation flow back into silent song, into inner chant, and hold and cherish that peace, hold that rising love in your heart and let it rise with you from your altar to spend the day in your Lover's presence.

CHAPTER 31

Of Brother Bhaktananda's Bliss

The Patron Saint of Flying

BROTHER BHAKTANANDA WAS speaking, as he always got round to doing, about practicing the Presence of the Divine, about inner chanting, and about the bliss that comes with it in time. He would tell us often of how his joy in this had grown through the years, of how he would take one chant and silently chant it throughout the day for several years until he felt great bliss, and then move on to another one and feel still greater bliss. When he was feeling great joy one day working in the garden affirming "I want to feel Thy Presence," one of the other monks called out to him that the Master wanted him on the telephone.

"So I went to the phone, and said, "Yes, sir?" And he said, 'Bhaktananda, are you happy?' And I said, 'Oh, yes sir, I'm very happy.' And he said, 'Oh, that's good!' and hung up! And I thought to myself, 'Now, that was strange! I wonder why he asked that?'

And within a few moments Brother Bhaktananda's happiness suddenly became very great indeed — so great that his body refused to obey the laws of gravity. He would tell us of this so humbly that people often missed what he was telling them. "So, I went in to join the monks at dinner, and I was feeling such great bliss and felt so light I just kind of leaped over the chair as I sat down. The other monks noticed this, of course. And then I went back out into the garden afterwards to work again, and there was this fence to climb, but I just sort of rose right over that, too. I learned to control it after a while. So you see, you can feel great joy in God if you practice this. It will come in time."

Of Stillness and a Bird

Once a young man at Brother's church was standing by a tree outside the monastery gate, with his arm outstretched, hoping by his perfect stillness to draw a bird singing in a branch above to fly down onto his arm. Brother Bhaktananda came by, smiled, and as he walked past, he observed, "You're not still enough!" and walked on through the gate.

The bird then flew down from the tree onto the ground and hopped along just behind Bhaktananda, following him into the monastery.

Bhaktananda's visit

Once a woman at the church was ill in the hospital for several months. She prayed to the Divine for healing, and focused on Brother Bhaktananda, asking for his prayers and blessings. One day, Brother strolled into her hospital room unannounced to see how she was doing. She was overjoyed to see him. They chatted for a little, and he assured her that all the monks were praying for her, and then he walked out. She immediately improved and was soon discharged from the hospital.

She went to the monastery to thank Brother for his visit. But he wasn't there – and had not been there for some time. She learned that on the day that Brother had visited her hospital room in Los Angeles, he was in fact more than five thousand miles away – in India!

Later, upon his return, someone asked Brother about it, but he wouldn't discuss it. "That's all Divine Mother!" was all he would say.

Brother Bhaktananda and William Tell

This story is a little strange. I hope I can tell it rightly so that you feel the eerie wonder of it the way I did.

I was asked to direct a play at Brother Bhaktananda's temple – a dramatization of a story from the Master's meditation lessons about a lady in India who wants to meditate but is always distracted. I was very pleased with the comedic bits I was inserting into the play, and was looking forward to lots of laughs at the performance.

Brother would sit in the back of the Hall, and watch rehearsals sometimes, and as I knew he enjoyed the plays, I was very hopeful of pleasing him.

There was one bit I was especially proud of. The lady who wants to meditate has let her little worries about her meditation pillow, and her ear plugs, and the comfy-ness of the chair, fritter her meditation time away – and then comes the final blow. The doorbell rings, she looks out the window with a horrified expression, turns back to the audience and exclaims, "Oh, no! It's my three gossipy girlfriends!"

In come the three girlfriends, who gossip madly away, killing all her meditation time. To show the rapid passage of time, I set up a strobe light that flashed in rapid-fire fashion, and the ladies made Keystone Cops-style silent picture "gossipy" motions, as a boy came out with a big clock that turned round and round rapidly, showing the fleeting hours go by. But, of course, we needed funny music! Nothing would do better, I was sure, than Rossini's "William Tell" overture – the famous "Lone Ranger" theme.

To my surprise, Brother objected. "The story is set in India. That music is not Indian," he observed.

"Well, yes, but you know, Brother, I'm sure it will be very funny!" I protested.

Romancing the Divine

"It's not Indian," was all he would say.

"Oh, but you'll see, Brother, it will be very funny. Besides, I've never heard of funny Indian music!"

I took Brother's silence for consent, and obtained a recording of the "William Tell" overture.

The next rehearsal, I came in early while the hall was empty to work with the sound and lighting technician on this sure-fire comedic hit. On went the strobe light, we hit the music, and oh! I could see that my comic masterstroke would bring down the house.

From the back of the hall came a voice. "That's right," said Brother Bhaktananda, "Get it out of your system!"

I turned round sheepishly, surprised to find him there.

"But, Brother, I'm sure it will really be very funny!"

He fixed me with a serious look.

"It may be funny to you," he said quietly. "But it's not funny to me."

This brought me up short. Something was going on here that went deeper than funny music, but I didn't know what it was. Brother was a man of few words, and he was able to read people effortlessly. I had no doubt that he knew me far better than I knew myself. But what was the problem? Something wrong with Rossini? Was it tainted by my ego? Was funny Indian music that important?

In the moment, I only knew that I was there to serve, and trusted his guidance. So I said, "OK, Brother, I'll do my best to find some funny Indian music."

But my mind was in rebellion, and my inner argument with him went on as I left the Hall to go back home. "Funny Indian music!" I snorted to myself. "Good luck! What's wrong with "William Tell" for crying out loud?"

To distract myself, I went to a movie, but I left after twenty minutes and walked out into the night on the Santa Monica Promenade to get some air, the argument over "The Lone Ranger" theme still going on in my head.

I looked up to see a ragged homeless man approaching me aggressively. The street was otherwise empty and a confrontation could not be avoided. He fixed his eyes on me, and stopped directly in front of me – and sang The Lone Ranger theme! "Ta da dum, ta da dum, ta da dum, dum, dum!"

Then he got right in my face and shouted at me, "What's your pleasure? Clean joke or dirty? Clean joke or dirty? Tell me! Which do you want?"

The hair stood up on my head. "Whoa, back up a second," I said, stepping back from him in shock. "Was that the Lone Ranger theme you were singing?"

"Yeah, yeah! Ta da dum, Ta da dum, Ta da dum dum dum! What's your pleasure, clean joke or dirty? Clean joke or dirty?"

I stumbled, and nearly ran in my haste to get away.

So what did it mean? Only a fool would dismiss it. Perhaps my "joke" was dirty with ego, or perhaps the music had a low vibration – the former, most likely. But the overriding impression of the incident was to let me know that if you have offered to serve Her, the Divine cares that you serve Her with surrender and humility, that She arranges lessons with loving and humorous detail, and that She will use anyone who comes to hand in order to reach you.

I never spoke to Brother Bhaktananda about the homeless man who sang Rossini. I found some funny Indian music, and the bit was a huge hit.

CHAPTER 32

▲▲▲

Saving the World

"Disquietude is vanity. Disquietude is always vanity. Yes, even if the whole world and everything in it were to be thrown into upheaval, disquietude on that account would be vanity."

- ST. JOHN OF THE CROSS

(Leading chants at an interfaith gathering sponsored by the Global Peace Initiative of Women during the United Nations Conference on Climate Change in Copenhagen, Denmark, December, 2009: left to right, leading Sacred Activism author Andrew Harvey, the author, Swamini Pramananda of Rishikesh, and Sister Joan Chittester).

Michael Henry Dunn

OCCASIONALLY WE HAVE a chance to put the great Spanish mystic's thesis to the test. This is such a time. World turbulence, financial crisis, personal upheaval - days when fear stalks your steps.

Is this a time to close your eyes and go within to seek the Beloved?

Yes. Now more than ever.

But would we not be of greater help to ourselves, to those we love, and to the planet if we were to turn our minds toward a cause of service, whether it be environmental healing, political activism, conflict resolution, or toward the urgent task of saving ourselves and our families from financial peril?

These questions may echo in your mind if you actually take the first steps toward intimacy with God.

They echo in my mind, too. They pose a false dichotomy - for can we not serve our families and humanity too, while enflamed with the love of God? But still amid the rising fears of these days these thoughts may haunt you as you struggle to experience the reality of Divine love.

They haunt me too, for I am a child of the Sixties, after all, and may be considered a fair representative of that idealistic generation. The heroes of my youth were (and in some cases still are) Dr. King, the Kennedys, Gandhi, and The Beatles. George Harrison spoke for many of us when asked in the mid-1990s whether the essential Sixties mantra "all you need is love" still had any relevance. "I believe it," said the quiet Beatle, "and I'm sticking to it!"

And then, too, being raised in the The Missionary New Age Church of Transcendent Mystical Irish-Catholic Tribal Holistic Medicine inculcated a sense of obligation to serve a greater good, to make a difference in the world. Being Irish Catholic, the Kennedy family was for us an inescapable presence in

Romancing the Divine

those years, somewhat to my father's chagrin, as he more than once observed that if we kids would only get our respective acts together, we could "make the Kennedys look sick."

Whether the Kennedys, God bless them, were ever actually very healthy was a question that did not arise.

And my mother would often preface a motherly admonishment with the phrase "what this world needs is for you kids to…(fill in the blank with the mission of the day)."

The implication being that the world needed saving, and that it was up to us to do it.

Now the world actually does seem to need saving. At the very least, you and your family may need saving. Of what value is pursuit of a romance with the Divine at such a time?

That depends entirely on whether you aspire to the highest or are content with mediocrity. It is clear to me, however, that you aspire to the highest because plainly you would not have come so far with me (Chapter 32 after all) on this most idealistic of quests if you did not.

If you choose to drift in the deep swift current with the rest of humanity, if you surrender the upstream struggle, and burden your soul once more with the delusion of an ego chained to a body, if you allow your beloved Source, your Mother-Father-Friend-Beloved, to fade back into a vague yearning mocked by your inner cynic, then you may experience a certain relief. You will be relieved of the weight of nobility, relieved of the burden of hope, and you may then turn your attention to the achievement of a delusive temporary security, the search for short-lived love, and the common struggle to stave off boredom until the oblivion of death.

Your material goals are of value. Create prosperity. Express your unique gifts. Take care of your family. But the soul yearning that prompted you to pick up this book will not go away with the achievement of such goals. Only "the highest" will satisfy that yearning.

Here, then, is what "the highest" looks like when it comes to being in love with God when the world appears to be falling apart - and especially when your life seems to be crumbling along with it.

If you go within each day to experience the peace of the soul and the love of your God, you will face that day with greater courage and higher joy.

If you realize through meditation that you are not, in essence, this body you inhabit, then you can play your part in this world and cheerfully discharge your duties to those you love, knowing that in the end you cannot lose, for you have allied yourself with that which is ever undefeated.

If hardship comes, you will face it with a calmer heart, and be better able to comfort others, and to pull through to brighter days.

If you have lured Divine Mother out of hiding, and have felt the warm touch of Her hand in yours, your heart may catch fire with desire to serve Her, and you may even be moved to speak of Her to others in whose eyes you see the same bleak yearning that once stared at you in the mirror. And Her vast drama of creation with its unavoidable defeats and certain victories will not shake your heart with fear, for you have seen through Her game, and will soon be in Her embrace.

And if you look on the pain in this world with an empathetic heart, and feel others' sufferings as your own, and you yearn to be of service, then She will place you where your gifts may do the most good, for She sleeps in the bodies of those whose pains you heal, and still it will always be only your Beloved everywhere you look.

Romancing the Divine

And this most of all: your careful nurturing of the growth of your soul's joy, the hours you spend in silence and in solitude, in intimacy with God, will be of more service to the world than the most heroic and globally applauded act of charity or peace-making that you can imagine. For the ripples that spread out from your purified life, from the countless unseen consequences of your loving influence, from the very vibration arising from the presence of one more God-knowing soul on the planet, may ultimately touch the lives of millions in ways that you will never know.

Or perhaps one day we will know. St. Paul did say, after all, that "eye hath not seen, nor ear heard…the things which God hath prepared for them that love Him," and it may be that a thrilling retrospective hereafter may wait for us, when we may see the ripples of love that spread out across the globe from even our humblest effort to hold the hand of the One who loves us all.

CHAPTER 33

Dark Night

"The worth of love does not consist in high feelings, but in detachment, in patience under all trials for the sake of God whom we love."

- ST. JOHN OF THE CROSS

BROTHER BHAKTANANDA TOLD us once that when you practice the presence of the Beloved intensely, and if the Divine comes to you as bliss, and if you continually go deep in meditation, that eventually you feel a constant bubbling joy within you – a joy you carry everywhere and at all times, despite trials and hardships.

And then he startled us. "Once it happened that God withdrew His presence from me for a time. But I didn't fret about it. God knows His business, and our business is just to love and serve Him."

Some of us were upset with the Infinite for this! Abandon our Brother Bhaktananda? How could God do such a thing?

We had instantly shrunk the omnipresent Spirit down to the level of a human lover who might come and go, who might flirt with the soul and then callously reject us – and it was ourselves we were worrying about, not our dear Bhaktananda! Brother knew, of course, that God was lighting up every cell in his body, was throbbing within as his very heartbeat – knew that the Beloved was in fact the essence of the love which he humbly offered back to the Beloved!

He knew that God could never abandon him, because the very idea of separation from Spirit was an illusion – an illusion we are here to unlearn.

To Bargain with the Lover

> *"He, then, is very unwise who, when sweetness and spiritual delight fail him, thinks for that reason that God has abandoned him; and when he finds them again, rejoices and is glad, thinking that he has in that way come to possess God."*
>
> - St. John of the Cross

When we begin to think we have won the Beloved, that the Lover belongs to us now, that the Presence will be there for us always in every moment, in every trial, then it often happens that the Infinite spies out in us a place of selfishness, or attachment, that needs to be tested, drawn out, and purified. And so it may be that we reach for the Divine Hand, and we suddenly do not sense a comforting response. We may plunge deep into prayer, and feel as if we are desolate and abandoned. We may look for the familiar Light in meditation, and find only darkness.

And sometimes this can go on for a very long time.

Mother Teresa of Calcutta received a blissful vision of Christ and a call to the life of service. Meditation and prayer were the bedrock of her life, but her letters have revealed that Christ withdrew His presence from her for *fifty years*.

Some have said that this means her life of great love and service was a sham. These are not matters in which we can presume to judge. My belief is that it is only the very greatest souls who are tested so severely. For Mother Theresa did not make a bargain with the Beloved, she did not fill out some saintly pre-nuptial contract in which she offered to serve the poor of Calcutta in Christ's name in exchange for regular visitations of Light and bliss.

Her love was unconditional.

She taught herself to see her Beloved in every dying beggar, in every starving infant, in every desperate mother on the streets of Calcutta. And her love endured.

In seeing the Infinite as our tender and true Lover, we must not think to have "our needs met" in the way we demand of a human love. There cannot be a bargain here – there can only be total love and total surrender. For in offering our love to God, we are asking not for human love that grows stale, or abandons us in death – we are asking for *everything!* Friendship that never dies, an ever-new joy that is continuously fresh, a Protector and Lover who will never leave us. And in return, we offer everything – all our love, all our strength, all our loyalty, all our service, for always – without condition.

The Reverend Mother, Sri Daya Mata, often told us that all she asks for in prayer is to be able to love her Beloved God ever more deeply, to be able to offer her love to the Divine.

That is all.

"Give!" she told us. "When you sit down to meditate, to offer your love to the Divine, waste not one thought on what you will receive. Give! Give! Give!"

When I have been pulled away by the world, by my duties, by my bad habits, and my life has grown dry and seemingly empty of God, Her response has been quick once I turn back to Her. She knows our hearts, and She knows if we truly want Her alone. It is as simple as the old French song, *N' Me Quitte Pas* – that is, as simple as the heartfelt cry, *'don't leave me!'*

But She never has left us. It is we who left Her.

When we first begin to seek the Beloved in earnest, the response is often warm and swift. I have heard more than one lover of the Divine tell of how in the beginning of their spiritual search, when they first applied themselves diligently to the practice of meditation, they were blessed with encouraging experiences of Light in meditation, of tangible and undeniable manifestations of the Divine as bliss, as peace, as love, until they were well on their way.

Then came the night for a while. The early encouragement was not a bait-and-switch...it was a gift. *'Now that you know I am Real,'* the Lover is saying, *'Seek Me! Earn Me! Find Me!'*

Perhaps This Is Not for You

Now this may seem too hard a matter for you, friend, and perhaps you are thinking this Path of the Lover might not be for you after all. Perhaps you are thinking that if you pay more attention to your career, or focus more on rebuilding your vanished retirement fund, or work on perfecting your attractiveness for that elusive dream lover, that this will be a better investment of your time than to spend hours in silent stillness and vague longing for the touch of an ethereal Lover who may or may not be real after all, and who might leave you in darkness for a time as a capricious test of your love.

You may choose to make one more bargain with the world, in hopes that this time, finally and forever, just maybe this once this time, the world won't disappoint you.

Don't get me wrong – I love the world! It's where my Lover lives. When the sun comes up it is no one else but Her. But it's just Her playground, and the game She invites us to is a cosmically playful and so very long drawn out Question Game – with only one question:

Michael Henry Dunn

"Do you love me?"

But if you've come so far in this little book, I will fondly imagine that you at least truly *want* to love God. That's all you need to begin. No step is lost on this path. And the Lover waits there, not at the end of the path to see if you endure, but at the very beginning, offering Her hand to guide your every step, if you will only reach for Her.

And as for the dark night?

> *Sunrise is good at arriving at the right time...*
> *All things must pass away.*
>
> - GEORGE HARRISON

CHAPTER 34

▲▲▲

Back to Assisi...and On into Darkness

W<small>HEN THESE PAGES</small> first began to appear, the dark night was still largely theoretical to me. I had struggled, yes, and been desperately sad at times. But I am a buoyant soul by nature, and I had never truly been brought to my knees in this life – brought to that existential edge where the light has faded, and doubt dominates, and a test becomes too severe to bear. When you first began to read these pages, we stood in the plaza of a hill town in Italy, in front of the statue of a dejected young St. Francis at the point of despair and transformation. I gave you the sense of an arc to this tale that would reveal how I too came to such a point. I am a storyteller and entertainer at heart, and I have shared many tales of sacred lovers with you, in my ardent desire to win hearts for the One I love, but I have left that arc unrevealed.

So now I will tell you briefly of my own darkness.

In rationalizing the pattern of modern marriages, it would be easy to recount the age-long history of the institution, and reframe it as an economic arrangement, a matter of dowries and negotiations, a tribal compact. It would be an easy point to make to note that only in recent centuries has marriage been saddled with the romantic expectations it now carries, and to excuse our divorces as the inevitable breakdown of an overburdened relationship.

But these rationalizations have not been my truth. I spoke sacred vows and I meant them from my heart. I vowed divine friendship that would transcend death. I vowed fidelity and truthfulness, anchored in a shared commitment that placed God above all.

Michael Henry Dunn

And I have left two marriages.

I carry the burden and blessing of having sprung from a union of true soul mates, of high noble spirits whose love for each other, for their children, and for their healing work in the world was of such power that the grace of it carried them through sixty years of sacred adventure and fulfillment. From my youth, I dreamed of finding such a mate, of blending love and mission, of bonding on a cellular level, of a twin-flame passion that would last an incarnation, of finding the lost mirror of my soul of whom we all dream.

My master, the world teacher and avatar Paramahansa Yogananda, taught that there is in fact such a reality, and that while we may have blessed companions in the journey of lifetimes, there is one twin spark in the cosmos with whom we must finally perfect the art of love. But as my fifty-second year approached, and the dream came to me prophesying flight and song and transformative death/rebirth, I had come to believe that there was no such mate in this life for me.

At that time all I knew was that the soul's fulfillment is beyond even such twin-souled love, that we all finally yearn for the eternal embrace. For still the old nun's gentle laughter haunted my heart – " there is no understanding this hunger for God above all." I knew that no mortal lover could carry me into that bliss, that the path is a solitary one that must be walked alone, though I might walk in companionship for some space of years.

Spiritual sanity lies in looking to one's own actions and thoughts as the matrix that gives rise to the life in which we find ourselves. Disease begins in blaming others, and hiding from growth. So I will speak my unvarnished truth as best I can.

My second marriage carried its own blessings and joys, and I will not dishonor the divine friendship I vowed by exposing the mutual failings that led to parting. I begin to learn now (just short of too late, I trust!) that I must look to my own part, and leave others' lessons alone. It was my choice to neglect my *sadhana* to struggle in a soul-killing business venture, my choice to fall prey to the national delusion that led the world into debt, my choice to accept community approval as a substitute for authentic spiritual depth, and my choice finally to walk away in one last quest to honor (as the beautiful novel "The Alchemist" calls it) my "personal legend" of a divine quest.

There is an unforgiving arithmetic in life from which I had been furtively hiding. Twenty-four hours, seven days, swift years, and a hundred seemingly small concessions to life's demands, and suddenly I woke one day to find that the world had me exactly where it wanted me: weary, distracted, and trapped, on the point of extinguishing the last embers of my heart's desire.

I had known for years that through my own choices I was on a downward spiral toward spiritual mediocrity. The devotional paths I have shared with you kept the Lover real to me, but I had come to accept a life in which we made ourselves busily serviceful in a meditation community...with little time left for meditation. Yes, I led meditations, recorded devotional chants that touched many, received much praise....and felt like a fraud. I had tried every remedy, and though I was still young and vital, I could feel myself turning into a bitter old man. I looked down the road, and saw a long slow defeat. Yet I could not bear to think of the pain I would cause by breaking free. I prayed many times that I might die before inflicting such agony. But our small home had become a cage of my own making in which I paced like a captive lion, or lay exhausted on coming home, as the thousand stresses of a failing business closed in around us.

I walked alone into the temple one night and sought privacy in the side chapel almost a year before the crisis of my departure. The darkened room was lit only by the small lamp illuminating the image of my master. Through long devotional habit, I folded my hands and bowed my head – and then collapsed on the floor, curled in a fetal position and sobbed like a child. The distance between the life of divine intimacy that I longed to live and the reality of the stressful façade that hid a grim struggle for survival was suddenly unbearable, and the thought came to me that this was as good as it might ever be in this life, that this stumbling sad striving was as close as I might ever come to knowing God. A middle-aged would-be divine lover lay there like a lost boy, body shaking with grief.

Do you think that the heart of God is not moved at such a moment? That comfort is not given?

Comfort was given. So compassionate, so tangible, so real, a physical touch as real as the caress of a lover, or the gentle rocking on a babe in the mother's arms. In a moment, She was undeniably present, touching first my hand, then my shoulder, where the presence lingered. I sobbed even harder to think that She'd been there all the while, and held Her hand fiercely. I did not yet know how I would be reborn, but the sublime reassurance in Her touch became a talisman that I clung to in the ensuing months.

A year later in Assisi I found the courage to leave, to embark on a terribly uncertain journey, to live alone again, to live in near poverty while affirming abundance, to endure the condemnation of my community for choosing to leave a marriage that others had thought to be ideal. The pain I gave was terrible, and the pain I felt was terrible. And there were times of fearful doubt and then despair.

So I can now speak of the soul's dark night in something more than an academic sense. Doggedness is perhaps my signal virtue - that, and a happy-go-lucky streak that borders on madcap — and I can only tell you that in the night it was a gambler's instinct in my soul that urged me to cling to that talisman of Her touch, even when monks and friends and ostracism told me I had erred.

And when the darkness began to recede, it wasn't to reveal a sun-splashed new landscape of rosy hopes, but rather a plain dish of lessons to be learned, new habits to be grooved in my brain, and a plentiful dose of humility.

Romancing the Divine

All along I believed that (if it came to it) I would rather *be* in love with God than be praised by others as such. So when the praise vanished and the condemnation came, I got to find out whether that was true. St. Francis' disciples, it is said, used to long for such tests, and one of them (on a journey of conversion to a region where his dialect was foreign) was so happy to be misunderstood by a crowd, so delighted at the spiritual test of condemnation, that he was about to contentedly let himself be hanged as a spy, until he was rescued at the last minute by a passing priest.

I won't pretend to have been so pleased at the condemnation, but grateful, certainly, for the rescue.

CHAPTER 35

The Lover in the World

THERE ARE TIMES when I begin to pray and I know my mind is not with Her. I speak the Name but my thoughts do not come home at the sound. And I know that if I let this go on, and do not find some way to stillness, I risk staleness in my love for Her, risk a habit of loveless repetition.

But if I can remember that She *is* the Name, that She *is* the sound, that my voice and my whispered prayer are themselves nothing but the trapped echoes of the animating song of love by which She made Life alive, made my thoughts, my mind, brain, and heart - and by which She sings the Universe anew from moment to moment and sustains its Being - if I can remember this, then the sound of my prayer, of my breath, of my heart, will bring me back to Her. All I need do is remember that my body is Her temple, is our secret meeting place, that the world itself is afire with Her presence to the farthest star. The instant I remember this, then my prayer at once lights with awareness of the Lover, and my breath is stolen by Her Love.

Her enemies do triumph sometimes. We do forget Her, we do get lost, grow weary, and find ourselves engaged in sins which (if we saw ourselves through the eyes that once brimmed with Her bliss) would make our souls sob with remorse.

Mercifully, however, She is everywhere, and cannot be hidden from. When you realize that you have forgotten Her for a time, have doubted Her for a time, merely remember that She is the Doubter, She is the Doubt, and that She was all the while more intimately one with you in the moments of your betrayal than you have ever been when united to the sweetest mortal lover you have known.

> "He who perceives Me everywhere, and beholds everything in Me, never loses sight of Me, nor do I ever lose sight of him."
>
> - THE BHAGAVAD GITA

Directions to Heaven

> *Your enjoyment of the world is never right till every morning you awake in Heaven ; see yourself in your Father's palace; and look upon the skies, the earth and the air as celestial joys; having such a reverend esteem of all, as if you were among the Angels. The bride of a monarch, in her husband's chamber, hath no such causes of delight as you.*
>
> *You never enjoy the world aright till the sea itself floweth in your veins, till you are clothed with the heavens and crowned with the stars ; and perceive yourself to be the sole heir of the whole world, and more than so, because men are in it who are every one sole heirs as well as you. Till you can sing and rejoice and delight in God, as misers do in gold, and kings in sceptres, you can never enjoy the world.*
>
> *Till your spirit filleth the whole world, and the stars are your jewels; till you are as familiar with the ways of God in all ages as with your walk and table; till you are intimately acquainted with that shady nothing out of which the world was made ; till you love men so as to desire their happiness with a thirst equal to the zeal of your own ; till you delight in God for being good to all; you never enjoy the world. Till you more feel it than your private estate, and are more present in the hemisphere, considering the glories and the beauties there, than*

Michael Henry Dunn

in your own house; till you remember how lately you were made, and how wonderful it was when you came into it; and more rejoice in the palace of your glory than if it had been made today morning.

Yet further, you never enjoyed the world aright, till you so love the beauty of enjoying it, that you are covetous and earnest to persuade others to enjoy it. And so perfectly hate the abominable corruption of men in despising it that you had rather suffer the flames of hell than willingly be guilty of their error.

The world is a mirror of Infinite Beauty, yet no man sees it. It is a Temple of Majesty, yet no man regards it. It is a region of Light and Peace, did not men disquiet it. It is the Paradise of God. It is more to man since he is fallen than it was before. It is the place of Angels and the Gate of Heaven. When Jacob waked out of his dream, he said, God is here, and I wist it not.

How dreadful is this place ! This is none other than the House of God and the Gate of Heaven.

- THOMAS TRAHERNE

For Traherne, the Beloved was at once the awe-inspiring Absolute and the touchingly present and loving Beauty of the world. This is what the Divine can be to us, if we will only look for Her there. Science can reveal Her workings, but leave us cold to Her presence unless we turn to the science of love. It is in your meditations that you can make the ultimate soul experiment that will prove to you in your very cells that She is Real. The ancient methods that the lovers of the Beloved have perfected over the centuries answer to the demands of science: repeatable steps that yield known results. For then we will find that Her presence in the world, in the Cosmos, is *our* presence, that (as my teacher said) spiritual realization is -

Romancing the Divine

"the knowing, in body, mind, and soul, that we are one with the omnipresence of God, that it is not merely near to us at all times, that we do not have to pray that it come to us, but that God's omnipresence is our omnipresence, that He is as much a part of us now as He will ever be. All we have to do is deepen our knowing."

PARAMAHANSA YOGANANDA

As we deepen that knowing, we begin to find that the Divine presence in the world greets us in times and places we never expected, that if we will only look for Her, the joy of recognition will leap up in our hearts at sight of an expanse of green meadow, of light on the water, at the secret glimmer of Spirit in the eyes of one you love.

CHAPTER 36

▲▲▲

The Passing of Brother Turiyananda

ANOTHER BOOK SHOULD be written about the life of Brother Turiyananda. But as I never met him, it is not mine to write. I walked up a holy mountain in the Himalayas one fine day in the company of a rascal Frenchman who could do a pitch-perfect impersonation of Turiyananda, and we nearly fell off the mountain laughing. I had heard recordings of Turiyananda, arrived at his home monastery just in the wake of his passing, knew a hundred stories of him, and I have met many who remember him vividly, so he seems almost like a memory to me.

But I will tell you a little of what I know of him, and of his passing.

Divine Mother was his great passion, and he was a man ruled by passion. He had run a biker bar in Switzerland before becoming a monk, and could never quite overcome his fondness for cigars, for motorcycles, for coffee of brain-jarring potency. He did manage to overcome the temptation of women, but only by being extraordinarily frank about it.

He was Divine Mother's bad boy, and in sermons he would speak of his struggles with such frankness and humility that the people felt that he was one of them, and yet holy too — that there was hope of bliss, if only one could love as deeply as Turiyananda loved.

He missed his Samurai incarnations, he said, and would wield his Japanese sword with great brio in his little monastic cell in the lakeside windmill. He was a man who demanded military-style obedience from the monks under his supervision, but was utterly humble and unpretentious. He

Romancing the Divine

would walk into a Santa Monica coffee shop and talk to strangers with unbridled enthusiasm about God, about his beloved Divine Mother. He could see the fine ethereal forms of fairies in the gardens, he said, and was known to blithely warn couples he was about to perform weddings for that one had murdered the other in a recent past life. He would wander into the garden visitors' center, airily telling gathered guests that you could tell the high sanctity of certain monks by the heavenly aroma that trailed behind them – while he hid a lit stick of incense behind his back.

Turiyananda was in the middle of performing an outdoor wedding ceremony in the garden one day, and the bride began to scream – the monastery cat had wandered under her bridal gown and become tangled in her fine under-things. "Don't worry!" cried Turiyananda, "I'll take care of it!" And he plunged enthusiastically into a search for the cat beneath the tangled bridal gown.

At a mountain retreat for the young boys one summer, an earthquake rattled the area. Afterward one rather rebellious lad, frightened by the experience, confided to Brother Turiyananda that he was afraid of dying in an earthquake.

"I wouldn't worry about it," Turiyananda counseled him brusquely. "You don't have good enough karma to die in an earthquake!"

He would discipline himself mercilessly sometimes, and once (half-seriously) asked the Reverend Mother for permission to have himself neutered so he would no longer be pestered by sex urges. (She reminded him with some exasperation that the body was not the problem!).

Once he fasted for a week, and strode out into the crowd after Sunday service – a crowd finely sprinkled with comely young women clad in Malibu's customarily scanty fashion for a fine June day – and gave one lovely young lady a terribly candid once-over with his expert appraising eye, whereupon he sighed heavily and said, "I look at you…and all I can think about is food!"

Michael Henry Dunn

Coffee was not allowed, but an exception was made for Turiyananda. "I promised Daya Mata I would drink only one cup a day," he said to some friends as he strolled the monastery grounds one day. "Only one!" He then held up an enormous beer stein - filled to the brim with the powerful muddy Turkish coffee that he loved.

He observed the monastery rules in the breach on occasion, and suffered from nostalgia for the European habit of wine with dinner. Once he told of a vision he had of the great saint who was his teacher, sitting across a table from him – on which sat a bottle of wine. The Master gestured to the bottle, and then to himself, as if to say, "which do you choose?" Whereupon, Turiyananda related, "I made a smart remark – and he vanished. But at least I saw my guru!"

One imagines the smart remark to have been something along the lines of "Why don't we have a drink and talk about it?"

He was still in vital middle age when he began to hint of his imminent passing. He began to give away all his possessions. When asked why, he said, "Because when they come into my room, and find me lying there dead, I want them to look around at my bare cell, and exclaim, 'what a great renunciant he was!'"

Against the rules, he allowed recordings to be made of his talks, and made a recording of himself reading love poems to Divine Mother. He would then listen to his own readings of the poems, and weep copiously at the beauty and the passion of it.

A close friend of mine who was a monk under Brother Turiyananda's supervision told me of his passing. "I lived in the room below him. That night, in the middle of the small morning hours, I heard in my sleep a thud on the ceiling above. Then Turiyananda came to me in a dream, and thanked me for everything I had done for him and for the shrine in the years we worked together. In the morning, he did not appear to give the Sunday service. We came into his

Romancing the Divine

room and found him lying there with a beatific smile on his face. The bliss in the room was so palpable you could barely breathe."

The grief at his passing was widespread and deep. Many who had come to the shrine only to hear him speak did not return. Sadly, they had come for him, and not for his Beloved.

After my French friend and I came down from the mountain in India, we joined the head monk at the nearby *ashram* in telling stories of Turiyananda. We laughed non-stop for ninety minutes. At length, the monk paused for breath and said, "You see? He was a saint. He has been gone ten years, and here we sit, laughing and blissful to recall his life."

CHAPTER 37

▲ ▲ ▲

The Beloved and the Fear of Death

THE JOURNEY OF death we make alone. No mortal friend or lover, no matter how faithful, can accompany us through that transition. Nor can they overcome their own passing to return to comfort us while we yet live.

Only the Lover can be with us now, stay with us through death, and guide us to whatever home awaits beyond it.

As we deepen our intimacy with the Divine, we find that our natural fear of death begins to fade. Experiencing the thousand responses that Spirit gives us in our most mundane moments throughout life, can we doubt that the Beloved will be there for us at the end?

And if we have made meditation a daily habit, we will have spent years experiencing the truth that the body is only a shell, a temporary home, that we are, in essence, sparks of the great fire of the Divine Consciousness of God, briefly tamped within the little lanterns of body-identified ego. And when death invites us to abandon the cage for greater freedom in Spirit, our animal fear, our primal drive for bodily survival, will have dwindled to a passing anxiety, and will fade as our souls loosen the knots that tie us here.

I could refer you to the studies on near-death experiences recorded throughout the world as proof of this. But why should you take their word, or the word of emergency room nurses, or the word of those who have revived, to convince you of your own immortality? And here, of course, I cannot give you testimony of my own, except my deep intuitive conviction that I am more than this marvelous bundle of nerves, and blood, and brain cells.

In candor, I must admit that I have a hard time getting very worked up about death: either my own or the passing of those I love – such is my blithe confidence about immortality. But I have not lost a child. I have not lost a beloved spouse. I have not seen a parent pass untimely, nor seen a young mother or father taken from young children. I have not witnessed the violent passing of so many who suffer sudden death in this darkening world. So do not take my word. Take the word of those who have passed through grief at its deepest and emerged closer to God.

Or take no one's word. Find the Lover. Feel Her presence. Know that She is with you beyond doubt, and then no word of mine, nor the word of anyone else will matter. You will live in the certain knowledge that you are every moment sheltered in the heart of a Friend who laughs at death to reach you, and whose love is beyond comprehension.

Preparing for the Passage

A truth about the Himalayas is that they can be a wonderful place to prepare for death. I do not mean remote sacred caves. I refer to the Indian bus drivers.

Before my journey to the foothills beneath the peak of Nanda Devi, I was assured by the tour director that my friends and I were very fortunate. "You are being driven to Dwarahat by our safest and fastest driver!"

The pairing of the two superlatives was not comforting.

In *The Bhagavad Gita,* India's most beloved scripture, we are told that "upon whomsoever one thinks in the moment of death, unto him he goes, in accordance with his nature." It behooves one therefore to cultivate the company of the Divine throughout life, so that your devotional habit will be so strong that when the supreme moment arrives, your heart and mind will be enwrapped in the thought of the Beloved from long practice. If you have gazed often into the Light of Spirit in meditation, your eyes will rise to that point effortlessly at such moments.

You may readily test yourself in this regard by riding a bus into the mountains in India. The drivers pride themselves on their combination of dexterity and bravado, and do not allow the narrowness of the road, nor the speed with which an oncoming bus of equal size is approaching them (with bare room on the road for one bus, let alone two) to persuade them to indulge in shamefully cautious behavior.

Observing this, I at first told myself that while it was terrifying, the drivers were used to it, and many things that would seem insane in the West were safely practiced in India. If one wants to hold to this delusion, it would be best not to glance too often at the bottom of ravines, where rusting hulks of burned out buses can often be seen at the bottom of the gorge.

On my trip to the mountain *ashram* I think it is safe to say that were at least two dozen moments when my eyes flew upward, and I clasped my hands in prayer, warning Divine Mother of my imminent arrival on the other side!

And where would I have gone, if my time had come, and I had held fast to the thought of my Beloved?

Where We Go
"In my Father's house there are many mansions," said Lord Jesus.

I am almost at the end of my tale, and I have done my best to speak from what I know. Here, of course, what I know I have forgotten! We have all passed many times through the portals of death — and back again through the portals of birth, so it seems to me. But the Divine mercifully blots out the memory of other lives, lest the woefully slow pace of our homeward progress should dampen our courage!

But souls I trust — souls whose truthfulness is beyond question, and whose lives bear witness to their deep spiritual realization — have spoken of the finer realms of light and energy to which we rise when we leave the denser vibration of earth behind — havens of rest where we are reunited with those we love, where we live with a freedom and a nearness to Spirit that can scarcely be imagined.

I do not want to distract you from the Beloved with quibbling over doctrine and theological concepts of afterlife. So let us say only this, with the Apostle Paul — he who told us that the joy he felt in Christ was so great that "I die daily" — he also reminded us of this:

> *"Eye hath not seen, nor ear heard, neither have entered into the heart of man, the things which God hath prepared for them that love Him."*
>
> - CORINTHIANS 2:9

What Do You Fear?

I was asked this question once by Sister Gertrude, a German nun at Rosary College in River Forest, Illinois. She was not being personally inquisitive, nor posing a theological conundrum — I was in German class, and we were all supposed to come up with an appropriate response in German, whether it was a confession of a terror of mice, or a great aversion to certain pastries.

My answer was one word: *Durchfallen.* Failure.

Michael Henry Dunn

Success can be defined a hundred ways, but failure is easy to describe. For me now, it would simply mean to look back on my life at the moment of death, and to feel that I had not loved enough, had not been grateful enough, had let pass too many moments of priceless opportunity to be of service, had failed to spread joy where I could, encouragement where I could, had neglected to gratefully express my gifts and to offer them in love to the Beloved.

Perhaps it is a residue of my upbringing in The New Age Missionary Church of Transcendent Mystical Irish-Catholic Tribal Holistic Medicine that I still worry about such things. But these worries are passing now, as they will for you too if you take Her hand often enough. I am Her knight errant – and Her knight erring! I have gone wrong often, and no doubt will do so again before it's over, but there is no longer any danger that I will finally let go of Her hand. And what more do I need to know, now or ever, than that She is with me?

CHAPTER 38

▲▲▲

The Reality of Bliss

I AM NOT a saint, just a longing and imperfect lover. I cannot speak to you personally of the blissful heights of union at its highest. I have been privileged to know at least three souls who can speak from such experience – a dazzling blessing, as such souls are rare. But with such bliss comes humility, and they would speak only rarely of this sacred reality. But I have come far enough on the path to recognize that they have simply reached a higher point along the way – a point that is nearer for me every day, though mercifully I don't know how far.

But we have this in common, these souls and I...we have all been taught and guided by the same great Teacher – my beloved and incomparable guru, Paramahansa Yogananda. And I will let that great one tell you of the heights of that blissful union with the Divine, when our longing to know Her has brought us to that place where "Knowing, Knower, and Known are one," of the love beyond love that awaits those who hold fast to Her hand:

> *An oceanic joy broke upon calm endless shores of my soul. The Spirit of God, I realized, is exhaustless Bliss; His body is countless tissues of light. A swelling glory within me began to envelop towns, continents, the earth, solar and stellar systems, tenuous nebulae, and floating universes. The entire cosmos, gently luminous, like a city seen afar at night, glimmered within the infinitude of my being. The dazzling light beyond the sharply etched global outlines faded slightly at the farthest edges; there I saw a mellow radiance, ever undiminished. It was indescribably subtle; the planetary pictures were formed of a grosser light.*

Michael Henry Dunn

The divine dispersion of rays poured from an Eternal Source, blazing into galaxies, transfigured with ineffable auras. Again and again I saw the creative beams condense into constellations, then resolve into sheets of transparent flame. By rhythmic reversion, sextillion worlds passed into diaphanous luster, then fire became firmament.

I cognized the center of the empyrean as a point of intuitive perception in my heart. Irradiating splendor issued from my nucleus to every part of the universal structure. Blissful "amrita," nectar of immortality, pulsated through me with a quicksilverlike fluidity. The creative voice of God I heard resounding as Aum...

- "AUTOBIOGRAPHY OF A YOGI"
PARAMAHANSA YOGANANDA,
SELF-REALIZATION FELLOWSHIP
LOS ANGELES

Perhaps such bliss seems too far beyond your reach for these words to stir your longing for it. And after all, I did not lure you here with promises of ultimate union with the Divine Ground of All Being - I spoke only of falling in love. But the One we love loves us too much to deny us anything, and Her greatest longing is that we finally be one with Her.

And being one with Her, is that the end? Is Eternity in love too much for our minds and hearts to receive?

I try not to trouble myself too much with such thoughts. There will be time enough to ask Her these questions on some other occasion.

I am grateful to you for reading these words. You and I are here – you holding the book and I writing the words - only because other souls who reached the Beloved paused on the threshold of Eternity, and came back for us. My prayer

Romancing the Divine

for you is that you will find the guide who is meant for you, who came back for you, who will place your hand in the hand of God.

Then all you need do is never let go.

Aum. Peace. Amen.

Appendix – Spiritual Resources

1. *(The book I found behind 'the Dwarf's Door.')* **Scientific Healing Affirmations,** by Paramahansa Yogananda, Self-Realization Fellowship Publishers, Los Angeles, CA. http://bookstore.yogananda-srf.org/product/scientific-healing-affirmations/

   This groundbreaking book reveals the hidden laws for harnessing the power of concentrated thought — not only for physical healing, but to overcome obstacles and create all-around success in our lives. Long before the use of affirmations was embraced in diverse mainstream settings as hospitals, recovery programs, sports arenas, and corporate suites, Paramahansa Yogananda understood and taught the deep spiritual principles that make this ancient scientific tool so powerfully effective.

   Includes comprehensive instructions and a wide variety of affirmations for healing the body, developing confidence, awakening wisdom, curing bad habits, and much more.

2. ***Autobiography of a Yogi,*** by *Paramahansa Yogananda, SRF Publishers, Los Angeles, CA. http://bookstore.yogananda-srf.org/product/autobiography-of-a-yogi-13/*

   Named one of the 100 Best Spiritual Books of the Twentieth Century, Paramahansa Yogananda's remarkable life story takes you on an unforgettable exploration of the world of saints and yogis, science and miracles, death and resurrection. With soul-satisfying wisdom and endearing wit, he illuminates the deepest secrets of life and the universe — opening our hearts and minds to the joy, beauty, and unlimited spiritual potentials that exist in the lives of every human being. This complete edition — available exclusively from Self-Realization Fellowship, the organization founded by the author — is the only one that incorporates all of his wishes for the final text including extensive material he added after the original 1946 edition and a final chapter on the closing years of his life. Includes 80 quality archival photographs. A spiritual classic that will help you discover the purpose of life.

3. *The Perennial Philosophy,* by *Aldous Huxley, https://www.amazon.com/ Perennial-Philosophy-Aldous-Huxley/dp/0061724947/ref=sr_1_1?ie=UTF8&qid =1514570057&sr=8-1&keywords=the+perennial+philosophy+by+aldous+huxley*

An inspired gathering of religious writings that reveals the "divine reality" common to all faiths, collected by Aldous Huxley.

"The Perennial Philosophy," Aldous Huxley writes, "may be found among the traditional lore of peoples in every region of the world, and in its fully developed forms it has a place in every one of the higher religions."

With great wit and stunning intellect—drawing on a diverse array of faiths, including Zen Buddhism, Hinduism, Taoism, Christian mysticism, and Islam—Huxley examines the spiritual beliefs of various religious traditions and explains how they are united by a common human yearning to experience the divine. *The Perennial Philosophy* includes selections from Meister Eckhart, Rumi, and Lao Tzu, as well as the Bhagavad Gita, Tibetan Book of the Dead, Diamond Sutra, and Upanishads, among many others.

4. *The Second Coming of Christ – The Resurrection of the Christ within You,* by *Paramahansa Yogananda, SRF Publishers, Los Angeles, CA. http://bookstore.yogananda-srf.org/product/the-second-coming-of-christ/*

In this unprecedented masterwork of inspiration, Paramahansa Yogananda takes the reader on a profoundly enriching journey through the four Gospels. Verse by verse, he illumines the universal path to oneness with God taught by Jesus to his immediate disciples but obscured through centuries of misinterpretation: how to become like Christ, how to resurrect the Eternal Christ within one's self.

Romancing the Divine

5. ***He and I,*** by *Gabrielle Bossis,* https://www.amazon.com/He-I-Gabrielle-Bossis/dp/0819834386/ref=sr_1_1?s=books&ie=UTF8&qid=1514570527&sr=1-1&keywords=He+and+I

   In this timeless spiritual testament, readers enter into the intimate, interior conversations between Jesus and Gabrielle Bossis, a French nurse and playwright. Recorded in her diary from 1936 to 1950, their tender exchanges capture Jesus' enduring presence in our daily lives, his insistence on kindly serving others, and his encompassing love for humanity--and show that ordinary individuals can experience an intimacy with Christ.

6. ***Self-Realization Fellowship Lessons,*** by *Paramahansa Yogananda,* http://www.yogananda-srf.org/PY_SRF_Lessons_for_Home_Study.aspx#.WkaINjdG200

   The *Self-Realization Fellowship Lessons* are unique among Paramahansa Yogananda's published writings in that they give his step-by-step instructions in the yoga techniques of meditation, concentration, and energization that he taught, including Kriya Yoga.

   The goal of these simple yet highly effective yoga techniques is to teach you to deal directly with energy and consciousness enabling you to recharge your body with energy, to awaken the mind's unlimited power, and to experience a deepening awareness of the Divine in your life.

   The *Lessons* were compiled under Paramahansa Yogananda's direction from his writings and the many classes and lectures he gave. In addition to his comprehensive instructions in meditation, the *Lessons* offer practical guidance for every aspect of spiritual living — how to live joyfully and successfully amidst the unceasing challenges and opportunities in this world of change.

   Each lesson is 6–8 pages in length, and is meant to be studied for one week. The entire course of *Lessons* lasts about 3 years.

Devotional Music

1. ***Adoration – Chants for Meditation,*** by Michael Dunn. https://store.cdbaby.com/cd/michaeldunn

   "This CD is WONDERFUL. I feel peaceful and so moved." - Mariel Hemingway.

   Sweetly intense and ideal for meditation - sacred chants and poetry in an angelic tenor, with traditional Indian instrumentation. Recorded by the author of this book in 2003, with the participation of fellow musicians from the SRF Lake Shrine Temple.

2. ***Light the Lamp of Thy Love – Devotional Chanting Led by Nuns of Self-Realization Fellowship,*** http://bookstore.yogananda-srf.org/product/light-the-lamp-of-thy-love/

   Joined by several thousand voices in an outpouring of devotion, the Self-Realization Fellowship nuns' kirtan group generates an atmosphere charged with the joy of God's presence in these live recordings from the annual SRF Convocations. Many favorites from Paramahansa Yogananda's Cosmic Chants are included, as well as several bhajans from India, providing more than two hours of inspiration on this collection. Includes a 14-page booklet with the words to all 19 chants.

Videos

1. ***Awake – The Life of Yogananda – A documentary film.*** http://bookstore.yogananda-srf.org/product/awake-life-yogananda-dvd/

   AWAKE: The Life of Yogananda is an unconventional biography about Paramahansa Yogananda, who brought yoga and meditation to the West in the

1920s. Paramahansa Yogananda authored the spiritual classic *Autobiography of a Yogi,* which has sold millions of copies worldwide and is a go-to book for seekers, philosophers, and yoga enthusiasts today. (Apparently, it was the only book that Steve Jobs had on his iPad.) By personalizing his own quest for enlightenment and sharing his struggles along the path, Yogananda made ancient Vedic teachings accessible to a modern audience, attracting many followers and inspiring the millions who practice yoga today.

Filmed over three years with the participation of thirty countries around the world, the documentary explores why millions today have turned their attention inwards in pursuit of Self-realization. Featuring interviews with direct disciples of Paramahansa Yogananda as well as with Ravi Shankar, George Harrison, Krishna Das, and many others. A visual feast taking us from holy pilgrimages in India to Harvard's Divinity School and its cutting-edge physics labs, from the Center for Science and Spirituality at the University of Pennsylvania to the Chopra Center in Carlsbad, California.

2. ***SRF Lake Shrine 50th Anniversary Celebration,*** *http://bookstore.yogananda-srf.org/product/srf-lake-shrine-50th-anniversary-celebration/ (This video features talks by Brother Bhaktananda and Brother Bimalananda, among other direct disciples of Paramahansa Yogananda.)*

On August 20, 2000, Self-Realization Fellowship held a day-long celebration to honor the 50th anniversary of the Lake Shrine's dedication. As part of the festivities, six monastic disciples of Paramahansa Yogananda shared informal reminiscences of their years with him and of events related to the opening of the Lake Shrine. This DVD captures their stories, interspersed with rare archival footage and photos from the dedication of the Lake Shrine. The inspiring accounts of these monks and nuns convey the love, joy, and wisdom they encountered in the great master's presence, giving viewers firsthand intimate insights into the experience of daily life around Paramahansaji.

Made in the USA
Columbia, SC
21 February 2018